Verses from Surrey
Edited by Mark Richardson

First published in Great Britain in 2008 by:
Young Writers
Remus House
Coltsfoot Drive
Peterborough
PE2 9JX
Telephone: 01733 890066
Website: www.youngwriters.co.uk

All Rights Reserved

© *Copyright Contributors 2008*

SB ISBN 978-1 84431 638 0

Foreword

Young Writers was established in 1991 and has been passionately devoted to the promotion of reading and writing in children and young adults ever since. The quest continues today. Young Writers remains as committed to the nurturing of poetic and literary talent as ever.

This year's Young Writers competition has proven as vibrant and dynamic as ever and we are delighted to present a showcase of the best poetry from across the UK and in some cases overseas. Each poem has been selected from a wealth of *Little Laureates 2008* entries before ultimately being published in this, our seventeenth primary school poetry series.

Once again, we have been supremely impressed by the overall quality of the entries we have received. The imagination, energy and creativity which has gone into each young writer's entry made choosing the poems a challenging and often difficult but ultimately hugely rewarding task - the general high standard of the work submitted ensured this opportunity to bring their poetry to a larger appreciative audience.

We sincerely hope you are pleased with this final collection and that you will enjoy *Little Laureates 2008 Verses from Surrey* for many years to come.

Contents

Sophie Cooke (10)   1

Brambletye Junior School, Redhill
- Elisha Mayne (8)   1
- Simon Ford (8)   1
- Julian Ramsay (8)   2
- Alexander Chalder (9)   2
- Aaron Humphrey (8)   2
- Megan Ford (9)   3
- Brendon Blyth (8)   3
- Abbey O'Byrne (8)   3
- Deanna Watling (9)   4
- Alex Pitts (8)   4
- Oliver Holmes (8)   4
- Maria Van Hoof (8)   5

Cheam Common Junior School, Worcester Park
- Chanel Macmillan (9)   5
- Rebecca Dove (10)   5
- Zainab Raza Bukhari (10)   6
- Ciara McEvilly (9)   6
- Emily McGowan (7)   7
- Azra-Jahan Hirji (9)   7
- Laura El-Bahrawy (11)   8
- Aaliyah Lawal (10)   9
- Chloe Dixon (10)   10
- Abbey Cattermole (10)   10
- Luella Marshall (8)   11
- Madison Nixon (8)   11
- Emily El-Bahrawy (8)   12
- Fazilah Riasat (8)   12
- Louise Pui Si Man (9)   13
- Harry Eates (8)   13
- Ryan Taylor (8)   13
- David Allen (7)   14
- Farah Baria (9)   14
- Libby Bradshaw (7)   14
- Fiona Murray Powell (8)   15

Hayley Bennett (8)	15
Sanjana Dawar (7)	16

Crondall Primary School, Farnham
Katie Harlow (9)	16
Peter Cusack (8)	17
Olivia Hardy (9)	17
Emily Ayers (8)	18
Harriet Rice (8)	18
Annie Coloe (8)	19
Hannah Morgan (8)	19
Phoebe Worthington (8)	20
William Passmore (9)	20
Olivia Pitcher (8)	21
Ella Smith (8)	21
Hollie Crowther (8)	22
Annabel Rice (8)	22
Holly Burdon (8)	23
Amy Hogg (8)	23
Ruth Wilson (8)	24
Christian Stoyanov (9)	24
Pearl Froud (9)	25
Laura Smith (8)	25
Marie-Claire Potts (8)	26
Alexander Carswell (9)	26
Ethan Butler (9)	27

Dunottar School, Reigate
Isabel Wood (7)	27
Annie St Marcus (10)	28
Freya Read (8)	28
Charlotte Hanwell (10)	29
Imogen Cliff (7)	29
Catherine Thomas (11)	30
Julia Lyman (9)	30
Charlotte Stewart (9)	31
Annie Smith (10)	31
Ananya Sengupta (9)	32
Lucy Robey (10)	32
Eleanor Durham & Georgia Bate (10)	33
Vicky Denny (10)	33

Georgina Smith (8)	34
Jessica Ferry (9)	34
Phoebe Daniel (8)	35
Yasmin Safar (11)	35
Harriet Sweet (10)	36
Rachel Brockman (10)	36
Ellie Gregson & Tara Hallam (11)	37
Emily Watson (11)	37
Gregoria Verity (7)	38
Jessica Richardson (9)	38
Becky Longstaff (9)	38
Amelia Terry (7)	39
Arabella Doorey (7)	39
Katerina Wintle (9)	40
Georgia Baker (10) & Chloe Barnes (11)	41
Lia Melconian (11)	42
Grace Hopkins (7)	42
Noshin Hussain (10)	43
Annabelle Terry (10)	43
Jessica Stoyle (10)	44
Emelia Troniseck (8)	44
Karolina Csáthy (10)	45
Gabriella Watson (8)	45
Sophie Shortland (11)	46
Aya Ali (8)	46
Rebecca Raeburn (10)	47
Emma Reynolds (11)	47
Catherine Huntley (11)	48
Mallika Khoobarry (11)	49
Brodie Musgrove (10)	50
Hannah Tiley (10) & Emily Boden (11)	51
Zoë Ross (10)	52
Georgia Lockyer (10)	52
Rosie Jones (10)	53

Horsell CE School, Woking

Amber Ruddle (8)	54
Ross Davidson (8)	54
Ben Jones (8)	55
Alina Reardon (8)	55
Louanne Spencer-Skeen (7)	56

Joshua Papworth (7)	56
Jennifer Leighton (8)	57
Amy Price (7)	57
Grace Fry (8)	57
Peter Haynes (7)	58
Megan Pawley (7)	58
David Faulkner (8)	58
Annalise Elgar (8)	59
Joseph Frean (8)	59
Jordan Creasey (7)	59
Lee Charman (8)	59
Sophia Lo Bue (8)	60
Robbie Faulkner (8)	60
Faaiq Malik (7)	60
Emma Florance (7)	61
Noemi Lampérth (7)	61
Thiana Aidoo (7)	61
Freddie Finn (7)	62
Cara Jones (8)	62
Ryan Ingham (7)	62
Sophie Lamont (7)	63
Ashley Lambert (7)	63
Emily Shields (7)	63
Elena Newton (8)	64
Jake Silverton (8)	65
Jack Stockdale (8)	65
Ami Fiveash (7)	66
Ewan Smith (8)	66
Mariya Farooq (8)	66
Elissa Avory (7)	67
Thomas Sellars (8)	67
Ben Coleman (7)	67
Luke Hall-Singh (8)	68
Richard Sugden (7)	68
Alex Zalaf (8)	68
Paige McElhatton (8)	69
Ben Goddard-Sheridan (7)	69
Shannon Blows (8)	69
Harri Jones (8)	69
Olivia Rhodes-Webb (8)	70
Miles Spiller (7)	70

Skye Chappell (8)	70
Catriona West (7)	71
Katie Clifton (7)	71
Usman Khan (7)	71
Richard Woods (7)	72
Joseph Lister-Mayne (7)	72

Manorcroft Primary School, Egham

Annabelle Laura Detain (9)	72
Jazmine Merrifield (10)	73
Sam Cutler (10)	73
Callum Cobb (8)	74
Grace Garland (7)	74
Tia Hilliard (8)	74
Kate Frank (7)	75
Shamilka Hewagama (11)	75
Yuvashree Venkatesan (7)	75
Rory Lee (7)	76
Samuel McLaughlin (7)	76
Ben Handley (8)	76
Michael Sparkes (11)	77
Dan Fitzpatrick (8)	77
Alex Andrews (8)	77
Sophie Lavender & Gemma Lapworth (9)	78
Rhiannon Warwick (10)	78
Holly Booth (8)	79
Emily Craddock (11)	79
Thomas Bückemeyer (11)	80
Chloe Bennett (11)	80
Joseph Spillman (10)	80
Maddie Lucas (10)	81
Robbie Loader (10)	81
Rosalind Down (9)	82
Megan Pointon (10)	83
Lucy Frank (10)	83
Clara Taylor (9)	84
Sarah Febry (10)	84
Rachael Baxendale (10)	85
Josh Ricotta-Legge (11)	85
Georgina Vlatas (9)	86

Sasha Purslow (7)	86
Samantha Dickens (10)	87
Rhiannon Stygal (8)	87
Bethany Mantle (10)	88
Jasper Dew (10)	88
Jack Tappin (10)	89
Becky Currell (7)	89
Leanna Gage (9)	90
Tabitha Finan (10)	90
Sonyusha Pandit (9)	91
Sean Lay (8)	91
Elvira Tahiri (7)	92

Oakfield Junior School, Fetcham

Oliver Doak (9)	92
Joe Guest (9)	93
Abbie Wright (9)	93
Joseph Charles Cooper (9)	94
Corin Hogan (9)	94
Sam Godwin (11)	95
Jessica Birks (9)	95
Tomine Paterson (10)	96
Thomas Popay (11)	96
Ellie Griffiths (10)	97
Sam Valente (10)	97
Brittany Attree (11)	98
Laura Harris (11)	98
Alannah Winn-Taylor (10)	99
Alex Stanbridge (10)	100
Yasmin Aziz (11)	100
George Warren (10)	101
Elliot Holman (11)	101
Georgia Eaton-Beddard (11)	101
James Adsett (9)	102
Elliot Woodhouse (11)	102
Abbie Hooper (10)	103
Katy Hart (11)	103
Helen Hutchinson (11)	104
Anna Rose Wyeth (7)	104
Nicole Sergiwa (7)	105

Elizabeth Anne Cole (8)	105
James Eade (9)	106
Joe Blunt (10)	106
James Cooper (9)	107
Lauren Morris (11)	107
Matthew Wilkin (10)	108
Megan Amis (10)	109
Megan O'Mahony (10)	110
Jacob Smith (10)	110
Sinead Robinson (9)	111
Devon McDonald-Howe (9)	111
Katie Harrison (9)	112
Sophie Way (9)	112
William Compton (10)	113
Sam Chamberlain (10)	113
Sam Leyshon-Garner (10)	113
Kimberly Stiff (9)	114

St Martin's Junior School, Epsom

Holly Seiver (10)	114
Kyra Litten (10)	115
Abi Cox (9)	115
Harry Symonds (11)	116
Rosabelle Armstead (9)	116
Joshua Eastwell (11)	117
Rhianna Miller (10)	117
Laura Sevenoaks (10)	118
Maryam Adil (11)	119
Laura Foxley (11)	120
Lydia Hallam (11)	121
Ruth Humphries (11)	121
Scarlett Soodhoo (10)	122
Olivia O'Brien (11)	122
Amy Ryckaert (10)	123
Sean Brown (10)	123
Darcey North (10)	124
Lauren James-Rikona (11)	125
Lauren MacKinnon (11)	125
Rachel O'Rourke (10)	126
Lizelle Johnson (10)	126
Danielle Owusu (11)	127

Stepgates Community School, Chertsey
Eleanor Charge (10)	127
Rudi Prentice (11)	128
Lewis Fry (8)	128
Peter Richard Robert Gerbert (10)	129
Charlena Ward (10)	129
Yasemin Carol Ann Kan (10)	130
Cheryl Jones (11)	130
Lewis Edward Hester (11)	131
Bethany Neville (9)	131
Bethany Aira (8)	132
Asma Khan (7)	133
Lauren Melvin (8)	133
Lillie Ella Derren (8)	134
Ellie Evans (8)	134
Charlie May Glue (7)	134
Mason Page (7)	135

Woodside Junior School, Croydon
James Ellis (9)	135
Martin Grady (9)	135
Georgia Doherty (10)	136
Seyi Joseph (9)	136
Ryan Grace (9)	136
Mason Ray Allen (9)	137
Joe Burgess (9)	137
Vanessa-Rae Harmony Williams (9)	137
Mason Glading (9)	138
Callum Harden (10)	138
Chelsey Moran (10)	138
Sophie Harrison (9)	139
Conor Wright (9)	139
Connor Moody (9)	139
Luke Majewski (10)	140
Rejoice Mpokosa (10)	140
Aimeé Fowler (10)	140
Alfie Cooke (10)	141
Scott Paul Wright (10)	141
Renu James (10)	141
Luke Diboll (9)	142
Isaac King (9)	142

Simone Gordon (9) 142
Helen Alemseged (10) 143
Katie King (10) & Lauren Foster (9) 143
Chelsea Couzens (9) 143
Abby Furmston (10) 144
Telka Donyai (9) 144
Luke Desmond James 10) 145
Rebecca Hooper (10) 145
Jamie Carr (9) 146
Sanjay Ravindran (10) & Sammy Kiy (9) 146
Daisy Boyle (10) 147
Ariana Andrade (10) 147
Bethany Jennifer Preece (10) 148
Ricky Parry (10) 148
Elgiver Mame Pramei Acheampong (9) 149
James Clayton (10) 149
Alex Wade (10) 150
James Whiteman (10) 150
Ellis Brown (10) 150
Joseph Bond (10) 151
Sheban Paramanathan (9) 151
Harry Jones (9) 151
Alex Isidoro (9) 152
Mia Brown & Bradley Sims (10) 152
Jarrad Soundy (10) & Matthew Hacche (9) 153
Samir Barakeh (9) 153
Joseph Simon (9) 153
Kobi Nanton (10) 154
Millie Meilhammer (9) 154
Jack Kingsnorth (9) 154
Surraya Chowdhury Jhane (9) 155
Dominic Richmond (10) 155
Alexander Thomas Polydorou (9) 155
Kayleigh Hannah Long (10) 156
Cheyeanne Nicholas (10) & Mollie Bailey 156
Ben Lockett (9) 157
Shaquille Stephens (10) 157
Emma Dewsbury (9) 158
Lucy Day (9) 158
Brandon Basquine (9) 159
Jasmine Holder (9) 159
Dominic Summers (10) 160

Georgie Jamés Newman (9)	160
Harvey Loundes (9)	161
Daniel Boateng (10)	161
Veronica D'Souza (9)	162
Sheneka Lindsay (9)	162
Brianna Janel-Lindo (10)	163
Kirk David Floyd Hutson (10)	163
Robert Willard (10)	164
Eleanor Clare Vincent (9)	165
Ellen Lawrence (9)	165
Ewald Hagan (10)	166
Henry Whiteman (10)	166
Dylan Offwood (10)	167
Jake Michael Lawrence (9) & Nathan Hall (10)	167

The Poems

Crimson

C herry-coloured poppies, scattered all over an emerald meadow
R ich, royal, ruby petals placed delicately onto a fairy's skirt
I ncredible blush roses, comfortably picked in a crystal vase
M agnolias stretching right up high to the sky
S carlet sprinkles, scattered into a rainbow
O utstanding blossom scenting the air
N ight falls, the flowers are hidden and asleep.

Sophie Cooke (10)

Emotions Poem

Fear is when I am in the dark.
Annoyed is when my brother kicks me.
Sad is when people call me names.
Nervous is when I meet new people.
Joy is when it is my birthday party.
Anger is when my brother laughs at me.
Silliness is when we are in the park.
Guilt is when I blame something on my brother but it was me.

Elisha Mayne (8)
Brambletye Junior School, Redhill

Emotions Poem

Annoyed is when people call me names,
Anger is when we make terrible noises,
Silliness is when we jump about everywhere,
Nervousness is when somebody is shy,
Sadness is when people cry loudly.

Simon Ford (8)
Brambletye Junior School, Redhill

The Cross Stitch Poem

B irthdays are fun and joyful
I s it fabulous or great?
R omanians have birthdays like England
T oo cool for school
H appy birthday
D ays like this are so cool
A mazing present, Mum
Y ou are so good at choosing presents.

Julian Ramsay (8)
Brambletye Junior School, Redhill

Fear Poem

Fear is when you are followed by a ghost,
Fear is when your house is on fire,
Fear is a roaring lion,
Fear is war, shooting and bombing,
Fear is your death flying to Heaven,
Fear will always be there to frighten you!
Fear is scary, ha, ha, ha, ha!

Alexander Chalder (9)
Brambletye Junior School, Redhill

Sharks

Sharks are predators when there are humans around.
Sharks can smell your blood from over 100 miles away.
Sharks are strong so don't mess about near them.
Sharks are around at sea in the winter.

Aaron Humphrey (8)
Brambletye Junior School, Redhill

Butterfly

B eautiful butterflies, red, green and orange
U mbrellas are different colours like butterflies
T ricks butterflies do are so amazing
T rying all they can
E verything they do is wonderful
R ed flowers they land gracefully on
F ly up into the sky
L ovely wings flutter up and down
Y ou see me in the garden and around.

Megan Ford (9)
Brambletye Junior School, Redhill

The Horrible Curse

In this most horrible land
There was a curse.
The children were scared
Living on a no good curse.
It was the worst you could imagine
With this terrible curse.

Brendon Blyth (8)
Brambletye Junior School, Redhill

Emotions Poem

Fear is when it is pitch-black at night.
Annoyed is when my sister hits me.
Anger is when I am bored as a bee.
Nervousness is when I start big school.

Abbey O'Byrne (8)
Brambletye Junior School, Redhill

Butterflies

Butterflies, butterflies everywhere,
Flying around here and there.
When all the boys and girls come out to play,
All the butterflies fly away.
Red, white, blue and green, rainbow colours everywhere.
Come outside to see them fly.
You can't catch me running away,
You can't catch me with your little legs!

Deanna Watling (9)
Brambletye Junior School, Redhill

Maths

Maths is when you add up sums,
Maths is when you have some fun,
Maths is when you add up numbers,
You add to ten, you add to hundreds.
You can times, you can plus, you can equal, you can add,
Maths is what you do when you add up sums.

Alex Pitts (8)
Brambletye Junior School, Redhill

Guilt

Guilt sounds like a volcano eruption,
Guilt smells like trouble,
Guilt tastes like you've done something terrible,
What does guilt feel like for you?
It's very frightening for me!

Oliver Holmes (8)
Brambletye Junior School, Redhill

My Monster

My monster is so cheeky,
My monster is so great,
My monster is so mysterious,
He ate up my best mate.

Maria Van Hoof (8)
Brambletye Junior School, Redhill

Christmas

C reamy cake on a full tummy
H oly people singing by the church
R oaring fire and roasting potatoes
I cy snowflakes outside
S teamy Christmas puddings
T asty turkey waiting to be eaten
M ince pies sprinkled with sugar
A ll of the presents to be opened
S ome snowmen being built.

Chanel Macmillan (9)
Cheam Common Junior School, Worcester Park

Christmas

C rackers cracking and echoing carols
H owling wind melting all the snowmen in its path
R oaring fire filling the house with warmth
I 'm inside eating crispy potatoes and turkey
S nowflakes outside as soft as cotton
T ree shimmering and glowing lights
M um making mince pies
A t Christmas I can't wait to open my presents
S nuggled up in bed looking forward to tomorrow, because
                                        it's Christmas!

Rebecca Dove (10)
Cheam Common Junior School, Worcester Park

Ode To My Brother

Oh bro, you are as humorous as a clown!
Whenever I'm lonesome you look out for me.
Oh bro, you're as squashy as the softest, whitest pillow,
You are a wrestler if somebody offends me.
Oh bro! Oh bro! Oh bro!
Oh bro, you are as sugary as mouth-watering chocolate!
You're a comedian whenever a friend or a relative is depressed.
You're as luminous as the bright blue sky.
Oh bro! Oh bro! Oh bro!

Oh bro, you're a soft, gentle swan
Who's good to play with on an overcast day.
Oh bro, you are just like a second dad to me!

Zainab Raza Bukhari (10)
Cheam Common Junior School, Worcester Park

Ode To My Dad

Oh Dad, you are a real role model,
You're as caring as a thoughtful animal rescue.
You give me delightful hugs that lovingly warm me all night.
I love you so much, I shall never leave you in my life.

Your hugs are as warm as a cat's fur,
Your talents inspire me all day long.
When I come home you are not there,
But in my favourable dreams you are always there
With your black shiny hair.

You're a hero of the town and my world,
You are really responsible to me.
Oh Dad, I would never replace you.
I love you very much and you love me very much!

Ciara McEvilly (9)
Cheam Common Junior School, Worcester Park

Roller Coaster

R oller coasters are big and scary
O nly sometimes you might get sick
L oop-the-loops are very frightening
L ightning stops the roller coasters and everyone is sad
E verybody can get scared on a roller coaster
R age is a roller coaster that I have been on

C ome on, let's go on that big roller coaster
O ur friends Rebecca and Sarah are roller coaster fans, just like me
A nd I feel really excited when it starts moving
S liding when we go down is fun
T urning round and round is one of the best bits
E ntering the tunnel is pitch-black
R unaway train is a really good roller coaster.

Emily McGowan (7)
Cheam Common Junior School, Worcester Park

Ode To My Bunny Rabbit

O dearest bunny, you are a gleaming light,
Shimmering on me on a gloomy, mystic and freaky night.
You're a lovely friend when in need,
You glisten at me like a golden seed.

You rub your eyes like wipers cleaning a windscreen,
As if you polish yourself.
Just like your eyes give me tranquility,
Preciously with trustful gleam!

I'm wishing to dedicate my whole life to you,
I love you,
So please come back to me.

Azra-Jahan Hirji (9)
Cheam Common Junior School, Worcester Park

The Last Day

I always stand here
Watching you.
I always see
What you do.
Not to me,
Not yet,
But I know my time will come.

You catch my eye,
I look away.
I've realised now,
You've chosen me today.
My head is spinning,
I can't get away,
But this is the last day.
I say, I hope, I pray.

But not, it has reached day two
And I'm becoming used to you.
I wait in the corner,
Sweating with fear,
Watching you
Coming near.
But this is the last day.
I say, I hope, I pray.

But no, it has reached day three,
Your threats are starting to get to me.
There's nothing to do -
But maybe there is!
This is the day *I tell Miss!*

She was ever so nice,
So kind, so caring,
And now, school life I'm bearing.
Now I have such loyal of friends,
Because the bullying has come to an end.

I walk past you during the day,
You won't talk to me.
I say, I hope, I pray.
But oh no! You do!
But what do you say?
'I'm sorry for bullying you every day.'

Laura El-Bahrawy (11)
Cheam Common Junior School, Worcester Park

Don't You Remember Me?

Don't you remember me?
I'm Cry Baby Carrie.
You said I was ugly
And I'd never marry.

Don't you remember me?
Your words pierced me like a fang.
Your friends have left you now
So you haven't got your gang.

Don't you remember me?
Your punches hurt with every blow,
Your kicks left me with scars,
You made me bow to you so low.

Don't you remember me?
Of course I'm famous - and rich
And you're begging on the street.
You haven't eaten for some days and you look like a witch.

Now you remember me!
You're scared but I forgive
Because if I don't help you now,
Like I did, you'll lose the will to live.

Aaliyah Lawal (10)
Cheam Common Junior School, Worcester Park

I Don't Know What To Do Today

I don't know what to do today,
Perhaps I'll go outside and play,
Or stay indoors and watch TV,
Or take a bath, or climb a tree,

Or maybe I'll go ride my bike,
Or pick my nose, or take a hike,
Or jump a rope, or scratch my head,
Or play a game, or stay in bed,

Or dance a jig, or pet the cat,
Or drink some milk, or buy a hat,
Or sing a song, or read a book
Or change my socks, or learn to cook,

Or dig a hole, or eat a pear,
Or call my friends, or brush my hair,
Or hold my breath, or have a race,
Or stand around, make up my face.

I'm so confused and bored and blue,
To not know what I ought to do.
I guess that I should just ask you,
So, what do you think I should do?

Chloe Dixon (10)
Cheam Common Junior School, Worcester Park

History

H istory that's the word
I nformation from the past
S hooting into my mind
T eaching me
O h what a glorious lesson
R eaching me into the past
Y esterday I knew nothing, today I know something.

Abbey Cattermole (10)
Cheam Common Junior School, Worcester Park

Cats

Cats, cats, cats,
I wish I was a cat.
If only I was black,
With whiskers, tail and ears.
Miaow, miaow, miaow,
I like to miaow.
Sitting by my bowl,
Waiting for my food.
Scratch, scratch, scratch,
I wish I could scratch
Upon the bedroom door,
To curl up on the bed,
Purr, purr, purr.
Can you hear me purr?
When my tummy's tickled,
I am a happy cat.

Luella Marshall (8)
Cheam Common Junior School, Worcester Park

TV

I come in from school and turn on the telly,
And get a snack to fill my belly.

I grab the remote and choose the channel,
Oh look, there's something on about a mammal.

I turn it over because it's boring
And find something to do with drawing.

I like it a lot because I like art,
It looks like a TV show called 'Smart'.

I turn it off to eat my dinner.
Who can eat the fastest?
Looks like I'm the winner!

Madison Nixon (8)
Cheam Common Junior School, Worcester Park

Cheating

I sat on the window sill,
Took off my shoes,
I went to play a game,
Thought I would lose.
When I got to my game,
Mum gave me a cheat.
When I had won,
My dad gave me a treat.

When they found out my tricky ways,
My brother was in first place,
I was in last place
For the biggest race.

Now you know what life is like
When you *cheat!*

Emily El-Bahrawy (8)
Cheam Common Junior School, Worcester Park

Time For School And Back Home

Reading book into my bag,
School diary into my bag,
Pencil case in my bag,
Time to zip my bag,
Lunch box in my hand
And off to school.

Time to go home,
Everything in my bag
And I put my school letter in my bag,
Then I go home with my mum.

Fazilah Riasat (8)
Cheam Common Junior School, Worcester Park

Work And Play

I work, work, work all day,
I work too much
So I don't have time to play.

I play, play, play all day,
I really shouldn't play too much,
I really don't know what to say.

Now this time I should do both,
Work and play, that's what I mean by both.
If I do both, I'll eat a loaf.

That's all good I see,
Brilliant, brilliant I tell you.
That's the end of me.

Louise Pui Si Man (9)
Cheam Common Junior School, Worcester Park

My Sleeping Bag

Soft, warm,
I play DS, I read and I sleep.
Will I ever get to sleep?
It only fits me.

Harry Eates (8)
Cheam Common Junior School, Worcester Park

My Bedroom

Bedroom,
Big, comfortable,
I play, I sing and I feel cool.
Do not come in,
It's all mine.

Ryan Taylor (8)
Cheam Common Junior School, Worcester Park

My Den

I like my den,
It's top secret and safe,
Away from everyday noise
With my favourite toys.

It's warm and cosy,
Hidden from everyone nosy.
If you know the motto,
You can come in my grotto.

David Allen (7)
Cheam Common Junior School, Worcester Park

Back To School

In the last week of the holidays
I was feeling glum,
I could hardly wait for school to start,
Neither could Mum.

Now we've been back a week,
I could do with a breather.
I can hardly wait for the holidays,
Teacher can't either.

Farah Baria (9)
Cheam Common Junior School, Worcester Park

The Sun

T he sun is really hot
H ot as fire
E nergy from the sun gives us electricity

S unny, sunny, sunny, sunny,
U nlike England
N o one could ever touch the sun.

Libby Bradshaw (7)
Cheam Common Junior School, Worcester Park

Nothing To Do

I sat on the window with nothing to do,
I went to bed, woke up brand new.
Took off my shoes, went downstairs,
Then I found my teddy bears.

Nothing, nothing, nothing to do,
I need a wee so I'll go to the loo.

I sat at the window in the hall,
It is very small.
Pitter-patter goes the rain,
Oh dear, what a pain.

Oh nothing, nothing, nothing to do,
I'll get out my dolls and I'll put on their shoes.

Fiona Murray Powell (8)
Cheam Common Junior School, Worcester Park

Ice Cream

Ice cream tastes mouth-watering, delicious and scrummy,
You eat it in a tall glass with a metal, shiny spoon.
Ice cream is colourful, fruity and sweet,
It comes in many different colours and flavours.
It looks icy, frosty and frozen.
Ice cream feels really sticky and gooey.
Ice cream is really tangy and tasty.
Ice cream is a treat.

Hayley Bennett (8)
Cheam Common Junior School, Worcester Park

Butterflies And Flowers

Relaxing with butterflies and flowers,
Away from the buildings and towers!
So many flowers on the ground,
Butterflies fluttering all around.
Tulips and daffodils dangling around,
Sunflowers and bluebells hanging down.
Bees and flies buzzing quite loud,
Butterflies make the children crowd!
Oh, what a pretty sight!
Won't you come and play outside?

Sanjana Dawar (7)
Cheam Common Junior School, Worcester Park

January

I see January as a young lady,
Soft as a blanket,
A white silky dress
With white shoes.
You could smell a roaring bonfire.
Her hair as black as darkness
As she steps into the room.
The floor turns into ice,
All slippery and slidy.
On the roof,
Icicles hang off.
Snow falling gently on the roof.
From the window, see the chimneys,
Step out of the room and feel
Cold, cold, cold, cold.

Katie Harlow (9)
Crondall Primary School, Farnham

January

A man by the fire,
Breathing heavily as he talks,
Telling stories of old times
When he was a boy.
Sitting in his armchair
When all the children have gone,
Slowly pulling on his fur coat
And blue scarf.
All nicely wrapped up warm,
He strides across the room.
Out of the door he goes,
Off to the newspaper shop.
Back he plods,
Hear his giant footsteps.

Peter Cusack (8)
Crondall Primary School, Farnham

January

A crying boy is by the fire,
But he wipes his tears away
For it is raining outside
And he wants it to be sunny
For all the children to play.
The taste of apple crumble
Fills the air with joy,
As you think of roast chicken
And parsnips,
And playing with your new toys.
February is approaching.

Olivia Hardy (9)
Crondall Primary School, Farnham

January

Stare out of the window,
See the black clouds cover the misty sky,
As the young lady of January
Slowly drifts nearer,
Her tears cover the world,
Pitter-patter on the rooftops,
Louder,
    Louder,
        Louder.

She scatters the dark clouds
Across the sky, then pulls them in,
Getting lighter and lighter,
Then fading away.
As she snatches them away
And throws them deep, deep
Down in her pocket,
She stretches across
The blue morning sky.
She drifts through the trees
Making them wave
Like a leaf in the breeze.
The spring is arriving!

Emily Ayers (8)
Crondall Primary School, Farnham

January

On a cold winter's day,
The wind as icy as an ice-cold cloth,
Leaves lie scattered, unknown as icicles get bigger.
Snow drifting down, but still trees are bare.
January is like a newborn baby as he hugs his mum
As they sit next to the roaring fire,
They hear the whines of children playing,
As bitter air flies past.

Harriet Rice (8)
Crondall Primary School, Farnham

January

January,
A sweet, beautiful lady, quite young.
Red lips, dark blue eye shadow
And eyes as blue as sapphires.

Smells all beautiful and new,
Like a new book should.
As fresh as a new year,
All because spring is near.

The atmosphere still,
Still as can be.
Quiet, quite scary actually!
No one is moving,
Everything is tense.
Nervous.

It tastes warm and strong,
But cold, bitter and icy,
Because of her power.

January is warm and fluffy,
But also freezing cold.
Finally she has to leave
Because February is approaching.

Annie Coloe (8)
Crondall Primary School, Farnham

January

January - a young lady,
Her cheeks as red as roses,
With bright green eyes and skin so smooth,
She brings a bright sun to warm us all,
A cheerful smile,
Sweet, honeyed breath,
Spreading a scent of a new year.

Hannah Morgan (8)
Crondall Primary School, Farnham

January

A cheerful old lady,
Wrinkled but kind,
Relaxed in her large green armchair
By the roaring fire.
Her voice was worn out
From all the cold winter days,
But feels excited
Like a brand new year is starting.
She smells of the winter's fresh air
Rushing to her face,
She sees the soaked, empty trees
Swaying in the breeze,
Like a hurricane racing past
On a cold winter's day.

Phoebe Worthington (8)
Crondall Primary School, Farnham

January

January is a very thin, tall man,
Wearing a long blue coat down to his heels.
Very pale, as pale as icy-cold snow,
With very white spiky hair,
Frozen blue lips
And icicles hanging from his nose.
But no, this is how it should be . . .

Raindrops like icicles fall and smash
Into iced puddles, splash, splash, splash.
Into the warmth of the fire comes a child,
A giant smile on his face
As he drops the presents, one, two, three,
He shouts out loud, 'Yippee!'

William Passmore (9)
Crondall Primary School, Farnham

January

A street child as unhappy as a homeless puppy,
With clothes ripped, cold and smelly.
Eyes weak and mouth trembles with sore pains hurting.
Hearing the wind howling his name,
Lightning striking,
If only a miracle would happen today.
A boy loved and cared about,
Clothes as soft as a fluffy cushion,
The smell of the new year and special treatment,
With friends and a lovely school,
Getting a giggle or two and a smile on his face.
January brings great news for some
And bad news for others.
So that's January.

Olivia Pitcher (8)
Crondall Primary School, Farnham

January

January - calm, breezy,
Like a new baby, ticklish and laughing,
Sometimes as loud as thunderstorms
Screaming through the window,
Sometimes as quiet as mice
Creeping through the house at night.
Kindness and softness
Filling the house.
Kind, friendly, clear,
Smelling of clean clothes,
Tasting like a butcher's and a bakery.
What else could there be?

Ella Smith (8)
Crondall Primary School, Farnham

January

January is like an old, ugly lady
Sitting in the damp, wet street
All alone.
The sound of the wild wind blowing,
The smell of damp dirt,
A rotten apple on your tongue.
The texture of rough dirt on her skin.
The atmosphere is like the bitter, cold air,
But people should really think of January as . . .

A young woman, beautiful as a peacock butterfly,
Brightly coloured and joyful as a puppy.
She sits curled up by the roaring fire,
As hot as the sun,
As red as a ruby,
Warming the damp day ahead.
Loud laughter rushing from her lips,
The scent of the new year,
The taste of a tingling on your tongue
Like roast turkey,
The atmosphere is like a smooth, silky dress,
Like the cosy feeling in a warm bed.

Hollie Crowther (8)
Crondall Primary School, Farnham

January

In the wet and dark, a cold girl stands,
Misty air whirling, swirling around her face
Like a small circle that never ends.
The taste of chicken caught in the air,
The little birds curling, twirling round
The great tip of the tree,
And a dark green blanket over the trees
That sway gently in the breeze
Awaiting the light and warmth of summer!

Annabel Rice (8)
Crondall Primary School, Farnham

January

A farewell from December echoes through a young child's brain,
He smells the fresh herbs of the new year in the cooking pot,
As the months start again,
His face smooth but fragile,
He lets out a firm stare
At the blazing fire ahead.
He soothes his newly-grown hair,
A soft feeling of upset and forgiveness returns to him.
He looks in wonder at children with presents.
At last, Christmas is over, January is cold and thin.
His voice like a million birds fluttering on high, icy mountains
Towering over the cornfields below -
Covered in a polar bear's coat of snow
Stretching for miles and miles . . .
January makes the ocean flow as he shakes out a silk curtain,
He lives for a thousand years it seems,
But for some he's cold-hearted and forgotten.
When he paces down the icy cobbled street,
Some clear white snow meets his feet.
He feels alive, before him his destination gleams!

Holly Burdon (8)
Crondall Primary School, Farnham

January

January is like a beautiful young lady
Strolling in the breeze,
Listening to birds singing,
Watching them curling and twirling
Round the tips of the trees.
She can feel the fresh air
Streaming through her hair
And the taste of roast chicken
Tingles on her tongue.

Amy Hogg (8)
Crondall Primary School, Farnham

January

A tiny, crabbed baby wailing
Is how they describe dear January.
With a small, wrinkled face
And a little red mouth,
Wet with rain and snow from mean December,
Lying in amongst the red and brown leaves,
Branches wailing and wind howling.
But there around her is the taste of dark magic
And the smell of something awful.

But no!
January should be a beautiful young lady,
With icy skin and a slim body.
She brings the tinkling breeze of spring,
The taste of the new year
And the smell of old Christmas.
Her breath, ice-cold as it catches the wind
And her small feet step lightly
Over the soft snow,
Her cheeks as red as roses.

Ruth Wilson (8)
Crondall Primary School, Farnham

January

A freckled, cheerful young boy
Dashing across the street,
Happily feeling the freezing wind
Blowing hard on his hands,
Tasting turkey with delicious stuffing,
While birds are singing very quietly,
Owls calling,
Cold icicles between your fingers,
Sliding in and out.
Bye to January, hello to February.

Christian Stoyanov (9)
Crondall Primary School, Farnham

January!

Winter has started, summer has ended.
My fingertips are frozen
And my lips are blue.
It's white everywhere.
I see an old man called January.
He has a grey beard
And smells of a new year
And old ragged clothes.
Winter is white snow all around,
Statues covered in ice like they have magic powers.
Now winter has started, and a new year.
Flowers end so new lives can grow.
It's wintertime and it will never go.

Pearl Froud (9)
Crondall Primary School, Farnham

January

Winter breeze brushing past your face,
Cold icicles hanging like lace.
Children scream in the cold, damp playground,
It's the sound,
Shouting and chattering of teeth
Reminds me of the owl's haunted screech.
January we always love,
It brings us hope of what's to come.
The fields full of flowers,
It's turning into spring.
Oh, the wonder which will come,
This song shall be sung.

Laura Smith (8)
Crondall Primary School, Farnham

January

January, as cold as wet snow.
A silver-light moon that shines and glows,
Like stars brightening the dark, cold sky.
Dinner tastes so scrummy and yummy,
Everyone likes it put in a bright bowl.
The leaves are wet and soggy,
Wrecked on the dirty floor.
The wind howling like a big scary wolf
Standing on the mountain,
Bending the trees over like they're falling.

Marie-Claire Potts (8)
Crondall Primary School, Farnham

January

January! The newborn baby
Celebrating the exciting new year!
Only spoiled by the grey-bearded man who smokes.
He smokes the pipe of the mist
And wears the hat of the rain,
The scarf of the wind,
And the gloves of the cold.
But both January, the old and new,
Promise a warmer, brighter future.

Alexander Carswell (9)
Crondall Primary School, Farnham

January

An ugly, young, excited boy,
Striding into the house,
Drenched in cold white snow,
Like polar bear's fur.
He sits down on a giant chair next to the hearth,
Groaning his displeasure of the coldness outside.
The icy air swirling round the cosy house.

Ethan Butler (9)
Crondall Primary School, Farnham

School

School days are back,
Science, history, maths,
They're all here
For all year,
For school.

I wish I was ill
And there was a bill
For school,

Then I would be free
And could watch TV
For school.

Everyone is thinking of school,
In town, country and Nepal,
For school.

Isabel Wood (7)
Dunottar School, Reigate

Snow, Snow

Snow, snow,
Fluffy and white,
Freezes your tongue
As you take a bite.
Cold white blanket
Coating the trees,
A beautiful sight
For you and me.

Snow, snow,
Gently a-falling,
Hear the wind gently a-calling.
Taste the frost that's cooling,
Feel the freeze that's coating,
See the snow that's sparkling white,
All through the day and all through the night.

Snow, snow,
What a lovely sight!

Annie St Marcus (10)
Dunottar School, Reigate

Coming Back To School

Waking up bright and early,
Seven o'clock, I feel poorly.

Coming back to school,
I hate it all.

Running in the playground,
Lots of noisy sounds.

End of the day,
Hip hip hooray!

Freya Read (8)
Dunottar School, Reigate

Smile

Injected into your heart,
Infecting your brain
With happiness,
Weather, rain or shine.

There is no exception to this feeling
As it travels through your body,
And all of a sudden
There is no reason to be sorry.

The things that you have done
Have passed through your thoughts
And suddenly you realise
There's no reason to feel distraught.
With everyone around you so forgiving,
The incident has been forgotten for a while
And suddenly on your face creeps a little smile.

Charlotte Hanwell (10)
Dunottar School, Reigate

My First Day Of Half-Term

One morning I woke up and shouted,
'Yeah, it's half-term!'
I ran out of bed, got changed
And ran downstairs.
My granny came downstairs and whispered,
'Why don't we start your Easter garden?'
I said, 'Yes!'
We found lots of things like flowers,
Pots, ivy and even some wood!
Reindeer moss, gravel, a mirror, Blu-tac
And also a slate wall and cinnamon sticks.

Imogen Cliff (7)
Dunottar School, Reigate

Thank Yous

Dear Gran,
How fantastic,
A Baby Annabelle,
Very different to my other presents
Like portable DVD players.
Can you tell me,
Is the crying supposed to stop?
Mum really hopes so.

Dear Great Uncle Ted,
Cheers for the Postman Pat CD,
With its cheery tunes.
Mum has insisted on keeping it
For a special treat for February.

Catherine Thomas (11)
Dunottar School, Reigate

The Easter Egg Hunt

Chocolate eggs are yum, yum, yum,
So come and join me in the fun.
The Easter bunny has come today,
So let's all shout, 'Hooray, hooray!'
Spring is here, the sky's bright blue,
Now it's time to read the clue.
We're not sure where to go, we're not sure what to do,
It's guessing time for me and you.
With squeals and shouts and laughing eyes,
We search about for a yummy surprise.
We run amongst the daffodils, we roll along the grass,
We search until we find a prize, at long last!
With buckets full of chocolate eggs,
'Can we eat them all now?' We beg and beg.

Julia Lyman (9)
Dunottar School, Reigate

My School Day

When I go to school
I find my teachers there.
I don't mind them really,
Though they give you too much homework.

Maths in the morning,
Starting work in the dawning.
Eight-thirty to three-thirty,
It feels like two days.

Screaming in the courtyard,
Whispering in the lessons,
Calling out in lessons,
Then getting told to shhh.

At the end of my school day
I go to see who's picking me up.
No one's there to pick me up,
So I walk along to waiting.

I know someone's there to pick me up.
With a grin on my face I go to the car
And I think, *what will I do on Monday
At my favourite school, Dunottar?*

Charlotte Stewart (9)
Dunottar School, Reigate

My Holiday

If I want to try some winter sports,
I'll need some snow of different sorts.
As well as that I'd like some sun
And a lot of friends to bring some fun.
To get the snow I'll have to go flying,
But I find flying very trying.

Annie Smith (10)
Dunottar School, Reigate

I Adore . . .

The things I adore are plenty,
Here, I will list a few.
Some treasures and some treats,
Some old and some new.

I love my Japanese mirror,
It sparkles and shines in the light.
If you glance at it for just a second,
You would marvel at the sight!

I relish tomato with omelettes,
And the rich taste of gloopy chocolate sauce.
I like pancakes and mozzarella cheese
And good ol' pasta - of course!

I enjoy drawing and painting
And making things as well.
Watching telly is great fun,
That's for sure, I can tell.

Best of all I love
All those who love me.
I hope that they may always
Smile with great glee.

Ananya Sengupta (9)
Dunottar School, Reigate

My Tree

Out of my window I see the leaves
Gliding as they float onto the grassy field.
Branches swaying from side to side.
The trunk stares at everything around it.
Branches point at me as if I am his worst enemy.
My waving leaves scattering to the ground quietly
And dancing as flying in the gentle wind.
They are yellow, they are brown,
Looking like gems on a crown.

Lucy Robey (10)
Dunottar School, Reigate

This Is The Story Of Lisa Clues Who Bought Too Many Shoes!

Lisa Clues had a craving for shoes,
She couldn't choose which ones to use!

One day her mother warned her that
She soon wouldn't have enough room in her flat
To keep all her shoes,
Oh the pinks and reds and yellows and blues,
Those are the colours of her fabulous shoes.

The next morning she opened her wardrobe door
And to her surprise the shoes fell to the floor.
She was knocked out instantly and she didn't see
They squashed her flat, I hope that doesn't happen to me.

And that shows that Lisa Clues
Shouldn't have bought too many shoes!

Eleanor Durham & Georgia Bate (10)
Dunottar School, Reigate

The Old Oak

As stiff as an old man's joint,
The oak tree's fingers reach to point.
The giggling, chuckling summer sun,
Laughing, smiling, a bundle of fun,
But the old, rigid, creaking oak tree
Wishes he could be free.
He dreams of running around,
But his roots stay grabbing the ground.
He stares at the younger trees waving and dancing,
And desperately wants to be skipping and prancing.
But he knows that dream will not come true,
And soon the skies will not be blue.

Vicky Denny (10)
Dunottar School, Reigate

Back To School

It was the day
I was going back to school,
It was terrible!

I went to the kitchen
To make myself poorly,
It was terrible!

My mum came into the kitchen
And saw me with chickenpox,
It was terrible!

All I wanted was
To go back to school,
It was terrible!

Georgina Smith (8)
Dunottar School, Reigate

K Is For Kestrel

Still hangs the kestrel there,
High in the still air
When the sky is fair.

So still he seems to stay,
He might in the fair day
Be fixed there far away.

But presently he will
Swoop from his airy hill
And make some small birds still.

Jessica Ferry (9)
Dunottar School, Reigate

I Love School

When I go back to school
I like it so much,
But in the morning,
I get a bit stressed.
Even though I can't
Get up in the morning,
I still love school.

When I go back to school
I enjoy my subjects,
But when I have to write a poem,
I can make a mess!

Phoebe Daniel (8)
Dunottar School, Reigate

Volcano, Volcano

Volcano, volcano when will you erupt?
Your lifespan is uncertain,
We cannot keep touch.

Volcano, volcano, the scientists say
It could be any time,
Night, year or day.

Volcano, volcano, magma lies inside you.
Volcano, volcano, the magma you can feel,
But we can't.

Volcano, volcano, we cannot keep touch.

Yasmin Safar (11)
Dunottar School, Reigate

Reader Beware, You're In For A Scare!

Haunted hotels are planted near vampires,
That is why we are all scared,
This I show we manage to put garlic in our rooms
And go to bed.
It all seems easy but I would like to see you try
Because you're the ones who are asking,
So come on then, tell me
Before you die!

I'm not joking,
It really is true,
And I know that because
It's about to happen to you.
Just before you go,
A quick note from all your friends,
A cross might do,
But be sure it's not you!

Harriet Sweet (10)
Dunottar School, Reigate

Guinea Pigs

Guinea pigs like to play all day,
Jumping and popcorning into the hay.

Whining, crying, squeaking and squealing to get their own way.
Running away when scared of the noise, but they seem to be OK.

They eat and eat throughout the day
Until they're full, then they can play.

Getting in a state, itching, scratching and sitting in the sun's rays,
Waiting for a bath to wash away the hay.

Rachel Brockman (10)
Dunottar School, Reigate

Sarah Deep, Who Spends All Day In Her Sleep

Sarah Deep was very fond of dreaming of things
Like James Bond.
She dreams of places
She never sees around
And dreams of faces.

She sleeps all day
And never goes to play,
With people that come round to stay.
She slept through breakfast,
Lunch and dinner,
She slept through her date
With Bobby Ginner!

One day when she got on the bus
She fell asleep
And woke up in a fuss,
As she found she had gone to . . .
China Town!

Ellie Gregson & Tara Hallam (11)
Dunottar School, Reigate

The Tree

The heavy roots are clinging tightly to the muddy ground,
Sinking lower and lower down, the roots creep.
The trunk standing tall like a straight soldier,
And branches tall like an old man's arm,
As it smiles softly in the gentle breeze.
Twigs pointing like witches' fingers at me, swaying fluently.
Leaves falling, dancing swiftly off the branches and
Onto the floor where pleasant children play in them.
Leaves fall from the top, dancing amazingly, like a beautiful ballerina.

Emily Watson (11)
Dunottar School, Reigate

Back To School - Bother!

I've got the school blues,
I just won't get up.
Then Mum shouts,
'Come down now, you're late for school.'
When I get down, I pack my stuff,
But guess what happens?
I go to school without having breakfast!

Gregoria Verity (7)
Dunottar School, Reigate

The Monkey

The monkey swinging
From tree to tree
Started to jump
Along with me.
We jumped, hopped, skipped
And danced as he came
Through the woods with me.

Jessica Richardson (9)
Dunottar School, Reigate

Dolphins

Dolphins, dolphins, splash, splash, splash,
There they leap, leap, leap, leap,
Dolphins, dolphins, splash, splash, splash,
There they swish, swish, swish, swish,
Dolphins, dolphins, splash, leap, swish.

Becky Longstaff (9)
Dunottar School, Reigate

The Last Day Of School

Yeah! It's the last day of school,
Tomorrow is the holiday,
I can have a swim in the pool,
I won't have to do maths nor English nor French,
Nor sitting on the old school bench.

It's lunchtime,
Yes it's nearly the end of the day,
I'm so speechless I don't have anything to say,
It's nearly home time now,
I can go home and play with my dog Pow.

It's the holiday,
Mum, what a great holiday we're going to have,
We're going to see Juliette,
And we're going to Bockett's farm,
And we're going to play in the barn.

Amelia Terry (7)
Dunottar School, Reigate

My Holiday

In I come, all cheerful and bright,
It's my last day of school and I am going out tonight.
I whizz through the day and hooray, it's my holiday.
I go to my friend's house, on the trampoline I hop and spring.
I go to the farm, in a big, big barn there was a duck and a baby,
                                                              baby lamb,
But wait . . . I am going back to school tomorrow.

Oh no! It's the dreaded day, I am not on my holiday.
I am now dragging my school bag into school
And I am working and working really hard,
But in four weeks everyone knows it will be my Easter holiday.

Arabella Doorey (7)
Dunottar School, Reigate

A Banoffee, A Muffin And A Banana Split

I eat banoffee, muffin and banana split,
So people think I'm a nitwit.
They never come around to play
Because they say that day they're away.

I had them nearly every day
Until one day they ran away.
My friends thought I was such a bore
Until Mum came back with more.

When I'm older I still will,
Even if it goes on the bill.
I won't care what my clients say,
Because I eat it every day.

Even if I were a bear,
I really wouldn't care,
Because I'll still have banoffee, muffin and banana split
And they may still think I'm a nitwit.

I still eat banoffee, muffin and banana split
And they can still think I'm a nitwit,
But I play with my friends nearly every day,
Even if they don't come round to play.

Katerina Wintle (9)
Dunottar School, Reigate

Angelica Gold

This is the story of Angelica Gold, who always got what she wanted.

There once was a girl called Angelica Gold,
She had more money than her pockets could hold,
She was such a spoilt, repugnant brat
That she had a mansion for her habitat.
Her little Chihuahua, Princess Pink,
Wore so many diamonds it made you blink.

Little Miss Gold was in her limousine
Going out for lunch at the Indian Cuisine,
But as she stepped out a robber passed by
And threw all her money into the sky.
But sadly the loot, it never came down,
And Angelica's face was stuck in a frown.

She ran home to her mum and dad
And for losing the money, her inheritance was forbade,
Now she lives out on the street,
Begging for money and a bite to eat.

If you lose your money,
You won't find it funny.

Georgia Baker (10) & Chloe Barnes (11)
Dunottar School, Reigate

Thank Yous

Dear Gran,
Thank you for the Dora Explorer doll,
It is very cute and can say so many phrases.
It is a shame it's stuck on one, 'Feed me'.
It's driving us all insane.

Dear Uncle,
Thanks for the book, I love the fairy pictures.
I read this book very quickly,
Seeing as it only has three pages.
How thoughtful of you.

Dear Auntie,
I am in paradise with the make-up you bought.
So safe to use, maybe because
It is for up to three's.

Lia Melconian (11)
Dunottar School, Reigate

Coming Back To School

I hate coming back to school,
You have loads of work after a lovely holiday.
Some people even have a smile.
When I go back to school I hope I'm in a dream.
My teacher is nice and my friends are nice,
But I hate coming back to school.
Oh I do wish everyone was home educated!

I hate coming back to school,
I think the best bit of the year is the holidays.
Every day when I wake up for school I'm grumpy.
Oh! I just can't wait till I'm a grown-up!

Grace Hopkins (7)
Dunottar School, Reigate

Whizzing

W hizzing up high in the sky as it shoots up with
    a yellow streak that flies by
H igh up in the sky it suddenly becomes pitch-black and then
I nstantly it pops, bangs, with all its exciting colours
    whizzing in different directions
Z ap and zoom, the curls and swirls go as the
    bright colours are soon to disappear
Z ip and all the colours are gone in a flash
I n a moment all the colours return with the same
    whizz, bang and pop
N ever do the colours stay the same,
    now it was a dark red and luminous orange
G leaming in its last moments, until yet another firework
    comes with a whizzing sound.

Noshin Hussain (10)
Dunottar School, Reigate

Autumn Song

Bonfire Night is a lovely autumn start
And is one of my favourite nights in the year,
Rings of fire which look like hearts,
Bangs and pops is all I can hear.

Catherine wheels that spin forever,
A glowing sparkle up above you,
Rockets which all whizz up together,
There's so many things that fireworks can do.

Fire burning in the sky,
The heat feels like a red-hot sun,
A glisten of orange in your eye,
It reminds me of a song being sung.

Annabelle Terry (10)
Dunottar School, Reigate

Thank Yous

Dear Aunty,
Thank you for my chocolate,
It was very kind of you.
What a shame it melted in the post
And felt like sticky glue.

Dear Uncle,
Thank you for my Arsenal shirt
That was made in 2003.
Though now it's 2008
And I support Chelsea!

Dear Grandma,
Thank you for my knickers,
How did you know I love pink and frilly?
Although they're not my size,
They don't look at all silly!

Dear Grandad,
Thank you for my sweets.
Although the tin was battered,
It was the best present that I got,
And that's all that matters!

Jessica Stoyle (10)
Dunottar School, Reigate

Back To School

Woken up at 7am,
By my sister's cry and scream,
Thinking about the school days now
And hoping Jack Frost has been.

So the pavement is really slippery
And all the schools have shut down.
That would be really cool,
And I would hear loud cheers from the children in town.

Emelia Troniseck (8)
Dunottar School, Reigate

Fireworks!

A light comes from nowhere,
A bang comes from hell,
When a firework bursts,
There's a smoky smell.

The vivid colours:
Red, yellow, green,
The night sky becomes
A cinema screen.

The rhythm of bangs
Stirs a wave in my head,
I can't get to sleep
Even though I'm in bed.

I'm glued to the window
Like magnet to fridge,
My eyes fill with sparkle,
I'm truly bewitched.

The dog can't stop barking.
Oh poor little thing . . .
Bang, puff, rustle, shoot!
Karolina Csáthy (10)
Dunottar School, Reigate

Lucky Morning

This morning I went downstairs
In my bunny pyjamas to find
A present sent from Granny,
She's very kind.
I had my breakfast,
I found a letter in my cereal,
It said, 'Hello sweetheart, you are to find
A little pressie under your bed,
Love from Aunty Meral.'
Gabriella Watson (8)
Dunottar School, Reigate

Thank Yous

Dear Sister,
How did you know I like soup?
The spoon you got me
Is perfect with the blue pattern.
It's just for me.
I love the way it's been flattened
So the soup slides off.
How clever of you.

Dear Uncle,
The Barbie you got me
Is so pretty.
The portable knickers, they're so hard to find.
How did you guess they're one of a kind?
How clever of you to think of me.

Dear Auntie,
The doll I got, it's naked.
How easy to put the nappy on.
It's a boy - how interesting.
It made me very happy.
Thank you, Auntie.

Sophie Shortland (11)
Dunottar School, Reigate

The Bully At School

On my very first day at school,
I went to my classroom and then came *boo!*
And that was the bully at school.
She scares everyone with the noise she made.
Oh no, that was the teacher coming through the door.
The door creaked very loudly and everyone was scared.
She came through the door.
Nobody made a sound, they just sat at the desk,
And we sat our best for the whole day.

Aya Ali (8)
Dunottar School, Reigate

What Am I?

I am happily relaxing on the soft sand
When all at once I am interrupted by someone picking me up . . .
Splash! I am soaked.
I hear people laughing and shouting and suddenly
I am being thrown about . . . oh, I'm so dizzy!
I see people relaxing on sunbeds and wish I was them.
I taste salt . . . *gulp, ugh!*
I just had a mouthful of salty water.
I feel the sun shining down at me sorrowfully.
Soon enough I am picked up by dry, warm hands
And placed on a sunbed.
Happily . . . now I can go back to sleep.
What am I?

Rebecca Raeburn (10)
Dunottar School, Reigate

Two Seasons

As I shudder in the wind
A golden carpet falls to the ground,
Of leaves and other things from trees,
Which then get spread all around.
My fingers stretch and I yawn,
Preparing for a new season,
But my lovely fiery coat has gone
And as I sadly wave it away,
Winter's coming nearer.
So I get ready for some cold, cold days.

Emma Reynolds (11)
Dunottar School, Reigate

The Tree

A soldier standing tall and straight,
Waiting to go into battle,
Its gnarled fingers catch you fast,
Soon it starts to shake
As one by one its golden plumes fall to the floor.

In shame the creaking figure
Acquires a new white coat,
Now very lonely without the birds
It quietly sinks back into the forest,
So sad in winter's depth it finally starts to sleep.

Now spring has come again,
All the little woodland animals come and play
In its adorning coat of silky blossom.
In its sturdy arms birds build their homes
As it watches over their young.

The hottest month of the year has come,
All kinds resting in the shade it bestows.
Soon its bloom turns to cherries,
Creatures squabble over their shares.
Many years I have been alive,
Enjoying the different seasons.

Catherine Huntley (11)
Dunottar School, Reigate

Guy Fawkes

As the bonfire crackled and spat,
I quickly put on my white woolly hat,
The smell of roasted chestnuts
Wafted through the chilling air,
Then I cuddled my little brother with tender, loving care.

Suddenly there was a blaze of scarlet and red,
But my brother could not see because of one very big head!
So my dad lifted him up onto his shoulder,
Then the big head did not seem like such a big boulder.

Finally the next one, it was purple and dark pink,
This one reminded me of a big splodge of ink.
I was then given a golden sparkler,
I looked just like my sister's toy fairy.
She had named it Mary.

We had a yummy snack,
Although soon it was time to go back.
I put on my pretty gloves
That were as white as doves,
Then we marched off back,
Right through the pitch-black.

Mallika Khoobarry (11)
Dunottar School, Reigate

Fireworks

I was in the factory,
I lay in pieces,
I waited on the conveyor belt to be put together,
The conveyor belt started, sj, sj, sj, sj!
I came out all sparkly and new,
I felt proud of myself.
I knew my time on this planet would not be long.

Ten great big sausage fingers picked me up,
I was packaged up in an enormous box with my friends.
The lid was closed,
I was in the dark,
I heard a vrooming,
I was moving.
I stopped.

I was in a lovely glass display cabinet,
I had some new friends,
I was not quite sure how long I would know them for.
Straight away some of us were bought.
I was the last one left,
Until a small little boy came to the shop,
That small little boy with his dad bought me with pride.

It was the finale,
Whoosh in the air I went,
I looked down at the boy who bought me,
I went *bbbbaaaannnngggg*.
Everybody clapped and cheered,
I was so very happy,
I was the finale.

This is my story!

Brodie Musgrove (10)
Dunottar School, Reigate

This Is The Story Of Bruce Who Never Did His Homework

One day there was a naughty boy
Who played and played with toys.

When he came home from school,
Oh how he acted such a fool.

He watched TV and rode his bike
And only sometimes he flew a kite.

He stuffed his face with loads of food,
And got his mum in a terrible mood.

He played on his computer, Xbox too,
And only stopped to nip to the loo.

One night his mum asked him if he had any work,
But he just smiled with a little smirk.

'Answer me!' screamed his mum.
'I don't get work, I'm way too dumb.'

'I'm going to look in your bag.'
'Sorry, can't, got to go and play tag.'

'That is it, you've made me mad,
You should feel extremely sad.

Come in Bruce, come in now,
You're in trouble and don't ask how.

You're going to be and I don't care.'
'But Mum, that's not fair!'

'I'm throwing away all your stuff,
You should be in a great big huff.'

He said, 'From now on I will try so hard
And here, I have made you a sorry card.'

So just remember before you play,
Do your homework every day.

Hannah Tiley (10) & Emily Boden (11)
Dunottar School, Reigate

Personification Poem

The soldier standing straight and tall
Shook his branches so the snow could fall,
Then he groaned and shivered some more,
How he wished that it was spring.
He wished that he could have his leaves back
And have shelter from the sun.
He was fed up of seeing white
And hardly seeing any light.
He wanted to be warm and cosy,
He wanted his cheeks to be rosy,
He wished that it was not so cold.
If only the sun could be bold,
Get the clouds out of the way
And come on out so they could play.

Zoë Ross (10)
Dunottar School, Reigate

My Bonfire Poem

Calm and gentle,
The bonfire was big, high and tall,
Filling the night with warmth and light,
Sparks flying everywhere,
The colours lit up the sky at night,
Dancing left and then right,
The flames forever strong.
The people, gazing up at the sky.

Georgia Lockyer (10)
Dunottar School, Reigate

Bonfire Night

Can you remember
The 5th of November,
When Alice went down to the park?
She had a big fright
As it wasn't so light,
In fact it was incredibly dark.

Orange sparks lit up the sky,
Gold, red, green and white,
Dancing up in the pitch-black sky.

The guy at the top was surrounded by fire,
As the flames climbed higher and higher,
And Alice watched him die.

Alice put her hands into her pockets
When suddenly up went the first rockets,
Screeching and screaming,
Whizzing into the sky.

Whoomph as they were lit,
Then you couldn't hear a sound,
Then suddenly . . .
Bang!
Thousands of colours high over the ground
And rained down
And disappeared by and by.

Rosie Jones (10)
Dunottar School, Reigate

Autumn

Autumn is like an orange and yellow blur,
Yes, an orange and yellow blur. Oh yes!
Autumn is a happy time,
We all play games and laugh merrily,
A happy time it is.

Autumn is like an orange and yellow blur.
Autumn is a bouncy time
With beautiful baby bunnies bouncing.
Oh how cute they are.

Autumn is like an orange and yellow blur.
Oh how pretty it is!

Amber Ruddle (8)
Horsell CE School, Woking

Autumn

Lovely autumn,
Sounds like rustling from the leaves.
Lovely autumn,
Reminds me of happy things.
Lovely autumn,
Smells like turkey.
Lovely autumn.

Ross Davidson (8)
Horsell CE School, Woking

Darkness

The sky is black,
Sometimes grey.

People hiding in the bush,
People hiding in the tree,
Robbers hiding everywhere.

The sky is black,
Sometimes grey.

In the dark
It feels like
You're alone
With no friends
To go to and
No one to play with,
No one to laugh with,
No friends to do
Anything with.

The sky is black,
Sometimes grey.

There's a smell in the air,
I don't know what it is.

Ben Jones (8)
Horsell CE School, Woking

Happiness

Happiness is golden like the sun.
Being happy smells like your favourite food.
Happiness sounds like children playing outside.
Being happy feels like the breeze in your hair.
Happiness reminds me of going on holiday.
Being happy looks like me playing with my toys!

Alina Reardon (8)
Horsell CE School, Woking

Holiday

Go on holiday,
Pack up your suitcase.
Go on holiday,
Don't fall down the stairs.
Go on holiday.

Holiday sounds like the sharks swimming.
Holiday reminds me of the butterflies
Hopping from flower to flower.
Holiday's like the nice hot air in your mouth.

Holiday is red or black
Because red is for the sky when it is hot.
Black is for the sky when it is night-time.
Holiday smells like the misty air wafting up your nose.
Holiday looks like bright sunshine in my eyes.

Louanne Spencer-Skeen (7)
Horsell CE School, Woking

Fantastic Summer

Yellow, hot summer air,
Summer is hot like the sun.
Yellow, hot summer air.
Summer smells like happiness.
Yellow, hot summer air.
Summer sounds like birds singing.
Yellow, hot summer air.
Summer looks like everyone is happy.
Yellow, hot summer air.
Summer reminds me of going to Legoland.
Yellow, hot summer air.
Summer tastes like burgers.

Joshua Papworth (7)
Horsell CE School, Woking

Autumn

Autumn is a lovely sight,
With leaves that fall off every night.
Leaves are fun, leaves are great
And pretty colours they all make.

Some are red and some are orange,
Some are as light as a feather.
When they go crunch, they sound very nice.
When they fall off the trees, they look beautiful.

Jennifer Leighton (8)
Horsell CE School, Woking

My Holiday

When I go on holiday it feels like I am on the sun.
It sounds like lots of children playing merrily in the park.
It smells like trees and fresh bread because it is near a bakery.
It looks like a beautiful street with lots of flowers.
Holiday's colour is blue like a swimming pool.
What a beautiful place!

Amy Price (7)
Horsell CE School, Woking

Winter

Winter makes me happy just like being clappy.
Winter is white just like snow.
Winter reminds me of Christmas.
Winter makes me glad because Rudolph the reindeer is out!
Winter tastes just like cold, bitter air.
Winter is fun because you get lots of presents from singing Santa!

Grace Fry (8)
Horsell CE School, Woking

Winter

Winter smells like chocolate,
Chocolate from the stocking,
The stockings were as green as frogs.

Winter tastes like turkey,
Turkey from the steaming kitchen.
The potatoes were hot as well,
Very, very, very hot.

Everyone went mad and sad.
Bing, dong, bong, they're here, they're near.

Outside the air was like ice-cold ice.
The weather however, was like ice and snow.

Peter Haynes (7)
Horsell CE School, Woking

Summer

Summer is multicoloured like birthday presents.
Summer is fun, summer is fun.
Summer tastes warm like a fire.
Summer is fun, summer is fun.
Summer smells fresh like clean clothes on the washing line.
Summer is fun, summer is fun.

Megan Pawley (7)
Horsell CE School, Woking

Feelings

Anger smells like stinky gas.
Anger is red like my face when I go red when I'm angry.
Worried is like learning to ride a bike.
Happy is like the sun shining on us.

David Faulkner (8)
Horsell CE School, Woking

Feelings

Anger is red like red-hot lava boiling up inside you.
Anger smells like the big flame of smoke coming off a bonfire.
Anger looks like a big, mean, fiery devil.
Sadness is blue like tears coming down your face.
Happiness is yellow like the big, warm, bright sun cheering you up.

Annalise Elgar (8)
Horsell CE School, Woking

Anger

Anger is red like lava from a volcano.
Anger is smoky steam as it blows out of the volcano.
Anger looks like a lava monster staring meanly all around.

Joseph Frean (8)
Horsell CE School, Woking

Anger

Anger looks like a ball of fire.
Anger is like fire from a dragon.
Anger smells like fire from a dragon burning rocks.

Jordan Creasey (7)
Horsell CE School, Woking

Happy

Happy is as green as grass,
Happy is like the moving ocean,
Happiness sounds like the owls hooting,
Happiness tastes like slimy, shiny snow.

Lee Charman (8)
Horsell CE School, Woking

Family Time

Family is the colour of gold
Glittering in the sunlight.
It looks all pretty like a heart
And it feels like love!
Family smells like lovely roses
And pretty little daisies.
It's as gold as the sun
And shiny too,
Family time for you!
Family fun like going for walks.
Come on everyone, join the fun!

Sophia Lo Bue (8)
Horsell CE School, Woking

Summer

Summer's sun shines on us.
On a summer holiday the sun shines.
Some of us go a long way, some go short.
Yellow is the colour of the bright sun
On a hot summer's day.
On a hot day birds tweet.
It's like a hot summer's day with a blue sky.

Robbie Faulkner (8)
Horsell CE School, Woking

Summer

Summer is hot,
Summer is good,
Summer is nice,
Summer is great,
Summer is beautiful,
Summer is the best!

Faaiq Malik (7)
Horsell CE School, Woking

Summer Break

Fresh summer air,
Clear beach water,
Fresh summer air,
The breeze is like the fresh air,
Fresh summer air,
How lovely can summer be?
Fresh summer air,
Oh wow, oh wow,
Can it be the fresh summer air?
Oh wow!

Emma Florance (7)
Horsell CE School, Woking

Summer

Summer is as hot as the sun,
As warm as your bed.
Summer is as hot as heat.
Summer's days are as green as grass,
We always eat salty salmon sandwiches.
You often think it's daytime
When it's time to go to bed.

Noemi Lampérth (7)
Horsell CE School, Woking

Winter

Winter is white like the glowing snow
On the floor by my house, all over my house.

Winter smells like a big turkey on a lovely Christmas Day
And a big chocolate cheesecake, as big as a box.

The winter is red like a Christmas bow,
Like the pointy, silky and straight parts on it,
When you open it and you touch the bow.

Thiana Aidoo (7)
Horsell CE School, Woking

Happy, Anger, Sad

Happy
Happiness smells like a piece of food that I like.
Happiness looks like the happy sun.

Anger
Anger smells like a dead rat.
Anger looks like a big, fiery red dot.

Sad
Sadness smells like a soppy tear.
Sadness looks like a big blue tear.

Freddie Finn (7)
Horsell CE School, Woking

Feelings

Excited is the colour yellow like
The sun is beaming on a girl called Geaming.
Sad is the colour blue like
Everyone is crying but some people are lying.
Looks like kids are having lots of fun in the hot sun,
But look there, people are crying a river of tears.
Excited smells like people are sweating and sweating.
Sad smells like lots of tears and it makes you cry
So you sniff and sniff.

Cara Jones (8)
Horsell CE School, Woking

Anger

Anger is red as fierce as lava.
Anger smells like red-hot boulders
From a volcano with some ash.
Anger looks like a fire god
From inside the volcano.

Ryan Ingham (7)
Horsell CE School, Woking

Feelings

Anger is red like a devil's horns.
Anger smells like a burning cigarette.
Anger looks like a poisoned apple.
Sadness is blue like falling tears.
Sadness smells like the blue sky.
Sadness looks like a cold ice wall.
Happiness is yellow like the shining sun.
Happiness smells like a kitten.
Happiness looks like a smiling girl.
Worried is purple like a dying flower.
Worried smells like a wet cloud falling.
Worried looks like a crying baby.

Sophie Lamont (7)
Horsell CE School, Woking

Anger And Happiness

Anger
Anger is red-hot like a fiery volcano.
Anger smells like smoke coming out of a cigarette.
Anger looks like a fire god in a volcano.

Happiness
Happiness looks like a sunset or a rainbow.
Happiness is gold like a summer's day.
Happiness smells like ice cream or strawberries.

Ashley Lambert (7)
Horsell CE School, Woking

Excited

Excited is gold like the boiling sun.
Excited smells like a delicious range of sweeties.
Excited looks like someone in a tree house
Eating chocolate biscuits.

Emily Shields (7)
Horsell CE School, Woking

The Night Sky

One night, some years ago,
I couldn't sleep.
I heard a funny sound,
It was an owl singing in the night sky.
The stars were shimmering all around
And the moon just stayed still all night.
The sky was dark, dark blue,
From where I was laying down in my bed,
In my dark, shimmering bed.
It got to six, there I was, still laying down in my bed.
It was time to get up.
I went downstairs,
The sky was still dark blue,
The stars were still shimmering
And the moon was still staying still.
When it got to seven,
The stars were gone,
The moon was going and turning into the sun
And the dark blue sky was turning light blue.
I went to play with my sister until it was time for school.
When we got to school
I went to play with my best friends.
We played 'It' as we always play,
We really like playing 'It'.
The bell went so we had to go in to class.
When we got in class, we were told
To do our two times tables up to thirty.
We always liked doing it.
When we had done that,
We had to sing a song that we were learning
It was called 'I'm OK.'
The teacher would always say it was
Showing we were OK how we were.
She was always right.
By now it was the end of school.
When we got home we had something to eat
Then we had to do our homework.
We didn't have much homework
So it didn't really matter.

When we finished our homework
We went to play with our toys
Until Mummy called dinner time.
We had beans on toast
And for pudding we had ice cream.
It was just turning eight,
It was time for bed again,
And that was the end of my day.
I had to go to bed then,
I'd got a big day ahead.

Elena Newton (8)
Horsell CE School, Woking

Football

We are lining up
Ready to go onto the pitch,
To get on and play.
Oh no, we're losing 1-0,
But now it's 1-1.
Hooray, it's a penalty.
Goal, it's 2-1 now.
Let's get off the pitch
And hold the cup.
It's great winning!

Jake Silverton (8)
Horsell CE School, Woking

Anger

Anger looks like the black side of the moon.
Anger smells like sweaty sweat
Mixed with dragon smoke.
Anger looks like a dragon
In a furious temper tantrum.

Jack Stockdale (8)
Horsell CE School, Woking

Feelings

Sadness
Sadness is blue
Like you're drifting off to sea and drowning.
Sad smells like salt in the sea.
Sad looks like you're hurting yourself
And your friend not helping you.

Happiness
Happiness is yellow like the
Sun shining on a summer's day.
Happy smells like getting
A special flower on Mother's Day.
Happy looks like a field of joy,
Or getting presents on your birthday.

Ami Fiveash (7)
Horsell CE School, Woking

Anger

Anger smells like flames
From a steaming pot of fire.
Anger looks like red-hot burning fire.
Anger's colour is red,
Like burning lava balls from a volcano.

Ewan Smith (8)
Horsell CE School, Woking

Anger

Anger smells like a flame of fire.
Anger looks like steam of hot lava
From a volcano bursting out.
All colours make me feel shiny,
Like the sun shining on me.

Mariya Farooq (8)
Horsell CE School, Woking

Anger

Anger is black like a deep, dark cave.
Sadness is blue like a puffy cloud.
Happiness is white like a soft piece of paper.

Anger smells like a stinky rat.
Sadness smells like a puffy sky.
Happiness smells like a birthday party.

Anger looks like a volcano erupting.
Sadness looks like an empty door.
Happiness looks like a fish in the sea.

Elissa Avory (7)
Horsell CE School, Woking

Happy

Happy is green like the green grass.
Happy is like a beautiful green tree.
Happy is like a green apple.
Happy is like a beautiful green bush.
Happy is like a green leaf.
Happy is like a green stem.
Happy is like a green cactus.

Thomas Sellars (8)
Horsell CE School, Woking

Excited

Excited is pink.
Excited looks like a sunny drop of rain.
Excited feels like a soft pillow.
Excited tastes like fish and chips.
Excited sounds like a quiet, soft, sunny pillow.
Excited smells like chocolate.

Ben Coleman (7)
Horsell CE School, Woking

Anger

Anger is red like burning magma.
Anger looks like a speeding tornado
With thunder and lightning around it.
Anger smells like fire burning away.
Anger tastes like electricity zipping around.
Anger feels like someone bounding around with anger.
Anger sounds like someone shouting rude things.

Luke Hall-Singh (8)
Horsell CE School, Woking

Anger

Anger is like hot, bubbling lava.
Anger reminds me of the hot desert.
Anger smells of steam.
Anger feels like hot fire.
Anger sounds like hot fire.
Anger looks like very hot fire.
Anger tastes like hot fire.

Richard Sugden (7)
Horsell CE School, Woking

Excited

Excited reminds me of a sunrise.
Excited is gold like money.
Excited tastes like strawberries.
Excited smells like raspberries.
Excited feels like swimming underwater.
Excited sounds like waves on a beach.

Alex Zalaf (8)
Horsell CE School, Woking

Anger

Anger is red like a fearsome dragon.
Anger tastes like fearsome fire.
Anger sounds like a hurricane or a tornado.
Anger smells like smoky flames.
Anger reminds me of fights and wars.

Paige McElhatton (8)
Horsell CE School, Woking

Happy

Happy reminds me of my best programme.
Happy smells like chocolate.
Happy feels like snow.
Happy tastes like a bath.
Happy looks like the sun.

Ben Goddard-Sheridan (7)
Horsell CE School, Woking

Joyful

Joyful is Chelsea winning the Cup Final.
Joyful is Chelsea scoring a goal.
Joyful is John Terry and Frank Lampard scoring goals.
Joyful is blue, the colour of Chelsea's flag.

Shannon Blows (8)
Horsell CE School, Woking

Excited

Excited is gold like you've just won the lottery!
Excited smells like salmon but it tastes like gammon.
Excited looks like a mic.
Excited sounds like the ocean rushing to your feet.

Harri Jones (8)
Horsell CE School, Woking

Sadness

Sadness is blue like the teardrops
That fall down my cheeks.
It tastes so cold and bold.
Sadness looks so wet and soggy.
How I really want a doggy.
Cry, oh cry, girl,
My mother says you will have one
In a couple of days.

Olivia Rhodes-Webb (8)
Horsell CE School, Woking

Angry

Angry is red like a boiling bed.
Angry's like a hot redhead.
Angry reminds me of my sister getting muddy.
Angry's like a person's annoying buddy.
Angry tastes like hot, beaming fire.
Angry sounds like a tyre screeching.
Angry looks like some hair bleaching.

Miles Spiller (7)
Horsell CE School, Woking

Happy

Happy is yellow like the shiny sun.
Happy tastes like a hot cross bun.
Happy feels like a big piece of clay.
Happy reminds me of when I go out to play.
Happy smells of flowers that are very cool.
Happy looks like a big swimming pool.

Skye Chappell (8)
Horsell CE School, Woking

Calm

Calm is blue like the sea.
Calm people never shout.
Calm people don't mess about.
Calm people never fuss
About things that don't matter much.
Calm people just sit and watch the clouds go by
In a great big beautiful bright blue sky.

Catriona West (7)
Horsell CE School, Woking

Happiness

Happy is yellow like the sun.
It tastes like we are on the beach.
It smells like seawater in the breeze.
It reminds me that you're on your summer holiday
Having fun, playing in the sun and
Splashing in the sea
Whilst the sun's reflecting over you.

Katie Clifton (7)
Horsell CE School, Woking

Happiness

Happy is yellow like the sun.
Happy feels good.
Happy reminds me of my dad.
Happy sounds like children playing games.
Happy looks like the sun.
Happy smells like the air.
Happy reminds me of my old school.
Happy tells me to be good.

Usman Khan (7)
Horsell CE School, Woking

Calm

It reminds me of falling asleep
At nine in the evening.
It smells like a summer's evening.
It feels like the wind in the evening.
It sounds like the leaves in the wind.

Richard Woods (7)
Horsell CE School, Woking

Cross

Cross tastes like vegetables.
Cross reminds me of lightning.
Cross feels painful.
Cross sounds like shouting.
Cross smells disgusting.
Cross looks red.

Joseph Lister-Mayne (7)
Horsell CE School, Woking

Elephants

Elephants have dry, grey, wrinkly skin.
When they're eating they make such a din.
They have pearly white, curved tusks,
They will be out till dusk.

With a swing of their trunks
They splash water everywhere,
You'll get soaked,
There'll be water here and there.

Rolling around
In their elephant way
On the dusty ground,
Every day.

Annabelle Laura Detain (9)
Manorcroft Primary School, Egham

The Disaster Week

Monday night, don't know what to do.
I don't know who I'm going out with, who knows who.
Tuesday morning, starving hungry,
Got no money, spent it all on a monkey.
Wednesday lunchtime, got the wrong bag,
In the shop I fell over a bean bag.
Thursday night, forgot my keys,
Next-door's dog has fleas.
Friday, nearly the end of the week,
It's been a disaster.
Saturday lunch, tonight got work,
My kids can't do their homework.
Sunday morning, the end of the week,
Now I don't feel I can speak.
Thank goodness the week is over,
Now, another disaster week.

Jazmine Merrifield (10)
Manorcroft Primary School, Egham

The Sea

There was a little fish
Who couldn't find his dish,
So he got eaten by a shark
Inside the sea park.

The shark was sad,
He couldn't find his dad,
So he went mad
And he went bad.

Then he started screaming
And the killer whale started beaming,
Then he started reaming,
Because he was dead!

Sam Cutler (10)
Manorcroft Primary School, Egham

The Cat Sits On The Branch

The cat sits on the branch
Of a gigantic leafy tree.
He feels tired and sleepy.
He takes a beautiful bird he sees,
He chases it up the tree
And then it flies away.
The cat sits on the branch
Of a gigantic leafy tree.

Callum Cobb (8)
Manorcroft Primary School, Egham

The Sun

The sun is sparkling,
The sun is yellow
And I am happy,
It makes everything warm.
When I go to Spain
The sun is waiting for me
And I am happy.

Grace Garland (7)
Manorcroft Primary School, Egham

The Sun

The sun is bright,
The sun is light.
I am yellow and
Shine everywhere.
I am up high
Where everyone can see me
In the sky.

Tia Hilliard (8)
Manorcroft Primary School, Egham

Sun

The suns' hot,
The moon's not.
The sun's big,
Dogs dig.
The sun is yellow
When the cat plays the cello.
The sun is round
The baby's just found
A toy of a sun.

Kate Frank (7)
Manorcroft Primary School, Egham

Feline's Foe

Drool dripper,
Tail chaser,
Bone ripper,
Ball fetcher,
Neighbour disturber,
Chaos causer,
Twitching nose,
Feline's foe.

Shamilka Hewagama (11)
Manorcroft Primary School, Egham

The Sunset

I am a sun,
I dance and play around the Earth.
I am hot, shiny, sparkly and bright.
I light up the Earth in sight.

Yuvashree Venkatesan (7)
Manorcroft Primary School, Egham

Autumn

Slowly, slowly,
The damp, dark leaves
Start to fall.
Looks like star shapes
With veiny lines.
Crease-shaped leaves
Start to pay us a call.

Rory Lee (7)
Manorcroft Primary School, Egham

My Sun

The sun is rising in the air,
Hot heating is fair,
No heating is not fair
And the sunny sun is bright,
And the world is round.
So sunny sun does not shine everywhere
And don't forget the sun is yellow.

Samuel McLaughlin (7)
Manorcroft Primary School, Egham

Mr Sun

Your light is so bright.
Mr Sun, you shine upon us all,
But in some countries, no light,
Because the world is round.
But you are still massive
And shine upon us all,
Mr Shining Sun!

Ben Handley (8)
Manorcroft Primary School, Egham

Jazz Jammer

Golden glinter,
Noise maker,
Button covered,
Jazz player,
Big nozzle,
High pitcher,
Low pitcher,
Breath taker.

Michael Sparkes (11)
Manorcroft Primary School, Egham

Spooky Poem

A creaky house with spiders,
Cold and wet,
Spooky noises falling,
It rattles night and day,
Roof leaking and it is leaning.

Dan Fitzpatrick (8)
Manorcroft Primary School, Egham

A Sunny Day

I am round,
I am bright, I am a light,
I am in the air, my name is the sun.
I power the winds,
I power the clouds and rain.
I make everyone smile.

Alex Andrews (8)
Manorcroft Primary School, Egham

The Haunted House

I was on my way to school today,
I think I took a wrong turn.
I came to a house all purple and black,
It made my stomach churn.

The house was surrounded by bats,
I thought it belonged to a witch.
I stared at it so much, you see,
It gave my stomach a stitch.

I wanted to see who the house belonged to,
So I knocked on the door.
There was nobody there,
Just a cat on the floor.

Then I realised,
No one lived there,
So I decided
To get out of the cat's lair.

Sophie Lavender & Gemma Lapworth (9)
Manorcroft Primary School, Egham

White World

Background blender,
Fish finder,
Sea swimmer,
Seal searcher,
Arctic animal,
Cold carer,
Safe sleeper,
White world.

Rhiannon Warwick (10)
Manorcroft Primary School, Egham

Tigers

Some live in African woods,
The others live free,
But if you go to India,
You may see me!

Trying to attract ladies,
Some are even called Hades.
Amazing stripes they possess,
Never even taking recess!

Climbing up the trees to find
Food to feed their darling wives!
Tearing off chunks of their food,
Even though they are arrogant and rude!

Tigers have some very foresty habitats,
I think they are very stripy cats!
Slender and beautiful they may be,
But to me they are just evil and mean!

Holly Booth (8)
Manorcroft Primary School, Egham

Silent Swooper

Occasional flapper,
Bony backer,
Low flier,
Meat eater,
Bare necker,
Circle overheader,
Black feathers,
Desert cleaner-upper.

Emily Craddock (11)
Manorcroft Primary School, Egham

Long Noser

Ground shake,
Four legger,
Tree pusher,
Water sucker,
Leaf gobbler,
Swish tailer,
Big fighter,
Long noser.

Thomas Bückemeyer (11)
Manorcroft Primary School, Egham

Fun Fur

Playful games,
Wet nose,
Fluffy ball,
Water hater,
Silent sleeper,
Fish lover,
Lazy lounger.

Chloe Bennett (11)
Manorcroft Primary School, Egham

Lizard-Like

Four-legged,
Ground crawler,
Rock sleeper,
Colour changer,
Rough backer,
Plant eater,
Big eyed,
Slow slitherer.

Joseph Spillman (10)
Manorcroft Primary School, Egham

Horses, Horses

Horses, horses everywhere,
Grey ones, brown ones over there.
Horses, horses, this way and that,
If they're good, give them a great big pat.

Horses, horses everywhere,
I ride and feel the wind in my hair.
I love to ride on a nice summer's day,
Then when she sees her food she goes *neigh*.

The end of the day, it's time for bed,
I make a bran mash and then she is fed.
She lays down and goes to sleep,
Before I go, I take a peep.

And then the day starts again . . .

Maddie Lucas (10)
Manorcroft Primary School, Egham

Dogs

I saw a massive dog, taller than a wall,
I was in the park playing football.

He ran towards my friend
As he slipped around the bend.

He licked my friend's head.
The dog's name was Fred.

I threw dog food,
I was in a bad mood.

They ran up the tree in the park,
We ran and left our mark.

It was a crazy day,
I'm glad everyone's OK.

Robbie Loader (10)
Manorcroft Primary School, Egham

The Cat

I have a cat,
His name is Pat,
He chases all the mice
When knocking down the rice!

He's a mammal like me,
Though he jumps high in a tree.
Then he climbs up the wall,
We all have a feeling he is going to fall!

When there is no fish
In his dish,
He makes a sound,
While scraping his feet on the ground!

When he's trying to catch a bird,
Without a single word,
He springs
And his bell rings.

His ears are as dainty as a flower
When he sits on top of his tower.
He sits on the mat
And chews my bat.
What a revolting cat!

I have a cat,
His name is Pat,
He is very fat,
But I love him loads and loads!

Rosalind Down (9)
Manorcroft Primary School, Egham

The Kitten

In the morning I opened the door,
Then a kitten came in and sat on my floor.
I sat down with crisps
And it suddenly hissed.
It sat on my lap
And I gave it a pat.
It curled up tight
As I turned to the right.

When it saw a fly,
It gave a loud cry.
You'd think it was cute
But I didn't care
Because it just sat there
With a tuft of hair,
But I still love it.

Megan Pointon (10)
Manorcroft Primary School, Egham

Standing Survivor

Wind dancer,
Berry grower,
Standing loner,
Land owner,
Arms swayer,
Weather survivor,
Leaf borrower,
Branch sprouter.

Lucy Frank (10)
Manorcroft Primary School, Egham

Food And Drink

Chocolate cake is yummy,
Pears are yummy too.
You can eat and drink
When you feel blue.

Every food is yummy,
Even ones that are hot.
Babies eat potatoes
In a little cot.

Water is quite nice,
But not always clean.
We get it for money
From the rich or mean.

I love to eat
And drink as well,
I think I'm in heaven,
Even if I fell.

Clara Taylor (9)
Manorcroft Primary School, Egham

Gas Guzzler

Gas guzzler,
Child nuzzler,
Window winder,
Baby minder,
Engine's cage,
Ice melt,
Sales dealt,
Tracks left.

Sarah Febry (10)
Manorcroft Primary School, Egham

Cats And Horses

The cat's fur is soft and silky,
It's longing for a stroke.
We feed it tuna,
But it hates a soak!

The horse gallops off in the distance,
Its mane is going wild,
It eats lots of hay
And likes the weather mild.

The cat purrs when it's happy,
Its tail wags when it's sad.
When it is naughty,
We say, 'Bad, bad, bad.'

The horse sleeps in a stable,
It gives you a ride,
But if it gets scared,
It hides, hides, hides.

Rachael Baxendale (10)
Manorcroft Primary School, Egham

Face Fighter

Ring reigner,
Glove gobbler,
Hasty hitter,
Jowl jabber,
Punch pinger,
Face fighter,
Fast flinger.

Josh Ricotta-Legge (11)
Manorcroft Primary School, Egham

The Weather Poem

Sunshine, sunshine very bright,
Makes your day very light.
Have a picnic, have a laugh,
Sunshine, sunshine very bright.

Rain, rain, wet and soggy,
Makes your day very boggy.
Stay indoors, play with your toys,
Rain, rain, wet and soggy.

Thunder, thunder, sharp and snappy,
Makes your day very clappy.
Clap your hands, stamp your feet,
Thunder, thunder, sharp and snappy.

Some days are very boring,
Makes you do lots of drawing.
Draw lots of pictures, draw round shapes,
Some days are very boring.

Some days are very fun,
It makes you eat lots of buns.
Eat, eat lots of sweets, do a little dance,
Some days are very fun.

Georgina Vlatas (9)
Manorcroft Primary School, Egham

The Apple

Apples, apples, good for your health,
Eat me all up,
I am very sweet and juicy.
I can be bright red and light green,
I gleam in the sunshine like a very shiny key.

Sasha Purslow (7)
Manorcroft Primary School, Egham

Swimming

Swimming is my hobby,
I do it every day,
I try not to be nervous
But it never goes away.

Swimming is my sport,
I train and train and train,
My favourite stroke is breaststroke,
It's easy, fast and plain.

My second stroke is butterfly,
Some people say it's lame,
Whenever I do training,
I train and it's a pain!

I do my galas well,
I never don't do my best,
I try to beat the others,
Sometimes I pass the test!

Samantha Dickens (10)
Manorcroft Primary School, Egham

Music

Music, music,
Fun to hear.
Music, music
In my ear.
Music, music,
It's the best.
Music, music,
Full with happiness.

Rhiannon Stygal (8)
Manorcroft Primary School, Egham

Summer

Summer is near,
The animals are here.
The sun is bright,
It's light at night.

Lots of pretty flowers,
Hardly any showers.
Lots of baby sheep
That I really want to keep.

I'll lie on a sunbed
Getting really red,
I'll soak up all the sun
While having lots of fun.

Summer's near,
I can't wait.
Let's have fun
Every day!

Bethany Mantle (10)
Manorcroft Primary School, Egham

My Friend, Tom

My friend is called Tom,
He's as funny as a comedian,
He always makes me laugh.

His hair is as dark as the night,
His eyes as bright as the sun.
When we play together,
We have so much fun.

Jasper Dew (10)
Manorcroft Primary School, Egham

Dogs

I walk on all fours,
I bark rapidly,
I don't have hands, I have paws.
Woof! Woof! Woof! Woof!

When someone throws a ball
I just can't resist it.
Whoosh! I am off, even though I am small.
Woof! Woof! Woof! Woof!

I always wag my tail,
I'm always full of joy,
And when I run in circles, I knock over the pail.
Woof! Woof! Woof! Woof!

And when it's bedtime I curl up by the fire,
Man's best friend I am,
Now you know what I am,
Goodbye, see you tomorrow! *Woof! Woof!*

Jack Tappin (10)
Manorcroft Primary School, Egham

Poems

I am going to a very good party,
I am going up the steps.
It is a very dark cave.
I got soaked in the rain.
I was looking for my homework book.
I can see a rainbow.
I am going down the steps.

Becky Currell (7)
Manorcroft Primary School, Egham

Food

Food, food, I love to eat,
Spaghetti, fruit, burgers and chips.
Food, food, so many choices,
Although most are nice, some are sick.

Exercise, exercise to keep fit,
Don't just sit on the sofa and eat, eat, eat.
Exercise, exercise to keep slim,
Cos I know some people who look like elephants.

I know, I know it's hard to exercise
When you have so much lovely food.
I know, I know, just have a go,
If it doesn't work, hit me real slow.

I've got a plan, I've got a plan, go and lay down, just exercise before.
I've got a plan, I've got a plan, just listen carefully,
Just get food you love, then sit on a couch,
Then watch High School Musical 2! Yo!

Leanna Gage (9)
Manorcroft Primary School, Egham

Hasty Hunter

Tyrannical leaper,
Benevolent predator,
Appropriate leader,
Good hider,
Sizzling body,
Burning stripes.

Tabitha Finan (10)
Manorcroft Primary School, Egham

Out In Space

Some children went out in space
And they had a long spaceship race,
Then they landed on Mars
And ate some chocolate bars.
The teacher said go to bed, so they did,
In a lid.
In the morning
The sun was dawning,
They had one more race
Out in space.
The teacher came first,
The spaceship burst
And landed on Earth,
The best place to be is the Earth.

Sonyusha Pandit (9)
Manorcroft Primary School, Egham

The Fire-Breathing Dragon

I am a fire-breathing dragon,
I have big wings so I can fly,
I have sharp claws and sharp teeth,
I have strong wings so I can fly.
I've got scaly legs.
So what am I?
A fire-breathing dragon.

Sean Lay (8)
Manorcroft Primary School, Egham

My Tree

I see a green and brown tree,
It is wonderful and massive too,
But at night it's creepy,
Just look at it smiling at me and you.
Birds at night stand on trees.
We're asleep.

Elvira Tahiri (7)
Manorcroft Primary School, Egham

My Cats

I have two cats,
One named Ella,
One named Blue.
Ella is black,
All silky and sleek.
Blue is grey,
All fluffy and cute.
Blue is always out and about,
Exploring, climbing and running about.
Ella prefers to stay inside,
Sleeping and snoozing instead of playing outside.
They're brother and sister
And are twelve years old,
But don't always do as they're told.
They jump on the beds
And make them all hairy,
Or run round the house,
Or curl up and sleep.
The thing that Ella and Blue love most to do
Is cuddle up on my lap and have a snooze.

Oliver Doak (9)
Oakfield Junior School, Fetcham

Into The Blue

You may think it's annoying
When you fall into the drink
And a squid squirts you with ink,
But stop to think.
It is just their way of saying, 'I'm scared.'
Squid, like most sea life,
Are more curious about us
Than we are of them.
I know that Jaws makes you scared,
But sharks can be beautiful animals.
They can be aggressive,
But that is only if they feel
You are threatening them.
So if you see a shark anytime soon,
Please remember to not just gawk open-mouthed
(Because you'll drown), just a figure of speech.
Keep to the edge of their territory.
Swimming with sharks is risky.

Joe Guest (9)
Oakfield Junior School, Fetcham

A Summer's Scene!

Covering the ground
Like a velvet gown,
Flowers grow all around.
On warm afternoons
I sit without care,
Whilst flowery smells
Magically fill the air.

Abbie Wright (9)
Oakfield Junior School, Fetcham

The Little Man

Little man on a tree
Sitting there so happily,
Wonder what it's all about?
Is he fishing for some trout?

The next day I saw the man
Driving an ice cream van.
I looked inside and saw the man
Cooking with a frying pan!

Every day I see the man
Doing things I don't understand.
Now the man has just begun
To start his flight to the sun.

I think his name is Mr Billy,
Isn't he so very silly?
He has a pigeon for a pet
And went to the moon for a bet!

Mr Billy's the little man
Living life *big* anyway he can!

Joseph Charles Cooper (9)
Oakfield Junior School, Fetcham

Crazy Animals!

Surfing dog,
Flying cat,
Mice that write,
Snakes that ski,
Crazy coo coos,
Hungry hamsters,
Pink panther
And busy bees.

Corin Hogan (9)
Oakfield Junior School, Fetcham

I Wonder

I wonder why the sky is blue,
I wonder why cows go moo.

I wonder why I can't drive a car,
I wonder why I can't drink in a bar.

I wonder why the grass is green,
I wonder why air can't be seen.

I wonder why my head is so thick,
I wonder if it's why I'm not very quick.

I wonder why I yawn and sigh,
I wonder why birds can fly so high.

I wonder why the moon rules the tide,
I wonder why the clouds float so high.

I wonder why a ball is round,
I wonder why moles make a mound.

Sam Godwin (11)
Oakfield Junior School, Fetcham

A Rat On My Head

I was asleep in my bed
With a rat on my head.
I woke up and said,
'Shoo, shoo, shoo,
And please go away
Because I'm scared of you.'
The rat turned his head and said,
'Please don't be afraid,
I only want to be your friend.'

Jessica Birks (9)
Oakfield Junior School, Fetcham

Gem Stones

I love gem stones,
They're so pretty and smooth,
Whenever I'm out looking,
They put me in the mood.

I love gem stones,
They're so groovy,
There are so many types,
Sapphire, jade and ruby.

I love gem stones,
Some white as milk,
They're so pretty,
Some smooth as silk.

I love gem stones
As you've seen,
I've been out looking,
Have you been?

Tomine Paterson (10)
Oakfield Junior School, Fetcham

Earth

E arth is round, it's where I live
A round it all is outer space
R evolving round the Earth is
T he sun and all the planets
H aving all the time in the world

E veryone is a star
A rriving to light up the sky
R olling round the Earth
T ime is very precious
H old on to it and use it wisely.

Thomas Popay (11)
Oakfield Junior School, Fetcham

Umbrellas

Umbrellas go up,
Umbrellas come down,
They circle round and round,
And maybe on a windy day
You too could get blown away.
They are used in all types of weather,
Rain, sunshine or snow.
It is always wise to have an umbrella
Wherever you shall go.

Posh young ladies have
Bright pink umbrellas,
Whilst gentlemen usually have black.
Mothers don't care what colour they have,
As long as it covers their hat.

Umbrellas go up,
Umbrellas come down,
Their coloured faces
Brightening up the rainy town.

Ellie Griffiths (10)
Oakfield Junior School, Fetcham

The Coin

As cold as a stone, the old coin
Round and flat, lies forgotten and dusty.
What is your past?
What is your future?
Were you swapped for a treasured item?
Were you a child's pride and joy?
Or were you a millennium memento,
Embossed, shiny and new?
We may never know.

Sam Valente (10)
Oakfield Junior School, Fetcham

My Horse Poem

I love horses very much

L ovely horses, horses I love
O ver courses of jumps we go
V an them or take them by horsebox to shows
E ating grass in the field

H orses are beautiful, they love to be nice to you and me
O h horses, oh horses, you love little treats so why don't you
                            have one and give one to me?
R acing through fields with other horses they meet
S illy, soppy horses dancing away. I watch them and they
                            come running to me.
E ating treats, apples and carrots they love
S o love them, don't hate them.

What does that spell?
I love horses.

Brittany Attree (11)
Oakfield Junior School, Fetcham

A Duck's Tale

Bobbing along with their pitter-patter feet,
Nibbling and pecking the plants,
Eating bread and quacking out loud,
As if they were happily chatting.
Swimming down the winding river,
Floating by day,
Sleeping by night,
Travelling under the drooping willows,
Their feet trail along the reeds.

Laura Harris (11)
Oakfield Junior School, Fetcham

The Girl

She does not cry
    Tears of salty water,
        She cries
            Deep maroon blood.

            She does not sleep
                On a duck-feathered pillow,
                  She sleeps
                      On her own hazelnut hair.

            She does not dream
            Of meadows in the golden sun,
        But frets
        Of the horrors lurking at night.

Her eyes are not friendly,
        Brown, blue or green,
            But haunted,
                Bloodshot and piercing black.

                Her skin is pale
            As the moonlit sky,
        Is shivering
        And growing cold as ice.

And as the owl hoots,
    A slow hollow call,
        She cries herself
            To a restless sleep.

            By dawn, it's a different story . . .

Alannah Winn-Taylor (10)
Oakfield Junior School, Fetcham

The Seasons

There the tree stands in spring,
Holding the cherry blossom to the pale sky.
On its head a nest crown with three pearly-blue eggs
Hidden beneath a blue tit sitting proud over them.
A young white lamb gambols under its outstretched branches.

In summer, its cloak of emerald green leaves covers the branches,
With fluffy white clouds above and lush green grass below.
The golden sun beats down all around the tree,
But it provides shade for all the small animals resting from the heat.

In autumn the tree's faded leaves turn to ruby-red,
Amber-orange and mud-brown,
They twirl and spin to the ground to rest with so many others.
As the sky turns dark and the ground grows muddy from rain,
You know winter is on its way.

In winter the wind howls through the bare branches of the tree,
With the snowy blanket upon the ground
And the frost sparkling in the morning sunlight.
The frozen pond nearby is twinkling in the light, like a shard of glass.
Nothing moves, all is silent, like a magical silvery picture.

And the cycle starts again . . .

Alex Stanbridge (10)
Oakfield Junior School, Fetcham

A Christmas Poem

The moon and the stars
Twinkling in the night sky,
The sound of bells
Floating so high,
Delivering presents to every house,
All people quiet, as quiet as a mouse.
As he falls from the chimney pot,
All the mince pies are gone in a flash,
They all disappeared as they were still hot,
I remember the night St Nick flew past.

Yasmin Aziz (11)
Oakfield Junior School, Fetcham

The Guinea Pigs

In our house there live some creatures
And these creatures have some amazing features:
A furry, glossy, tortoiseshell coat,
Gleaming, glistening eyes so bright that they could guide a boat.
When they're hungry they will squeak and squeal,
All they want to do is eat a meal.
When they're in a playful mood,
They'll run around and have some food.
And lastly, when they need a rest,
They'll go lay down in their nest,
And all I can say is what a pest!

George Warren (10)
Oakfield Junior School, Fetcham

Athletics

Athletics is fun because you get to run
And you might have won.
At competitions you might meet a famous runner
And when you do the relay, you have your friends with you.
And if you don't like running, we've got long jump and javelin.

Elliot Holman (11)
Oakfield Junior School, Fetcham

I Love Chocolate

I love chocolate, especially mint,
And occasionally I like to have Lindt.
I like to have it every day,
But only if my mum says OK.
I also like Twixes and Mars,
And sometimes I eat some chocolate stars!

Georgia Eaton-Beddard (11)
Oakfield Junior School, Fetcham

My Fishing Dream

When I lay in bed at night
I hug my teddy really tight.

Then the Dream Master takes me away,
In my bed I no longer lay.

Off through space and time
To dreams that are only mine.

Roach, rudd and perch lay in wait,
Maggots, bread and worms are my bait.

Bobbing float, I take a strike,
This one puts up quite a fight.

On my lap it flips and flaps,
It must be time to put it back.

Flowing rivers, misty lakes,
Silent ponds, can't stay too late.

James Adsett (9)
Oakfield Junior School, Fetcham

The Game

Rugby is a tough game,
Playing for England wins you fame.
Slippery mud flies through the air,
A shirt has a massive tear.
The crowd screaming and cheering with pleasure,
The team seem to have found their measure.
Fighting hard to win the ball,
Watching as grown men fall.
The game is over,
The team has lost,
At what cost?

Elliot Woodhouse (11)
Oakfield Junior School, Fetcham

All My Life

I sat in a belly, very warm,
I sat there waiting till I was born.
My mummy waited impatiently,
She wanted to see what I would be.

The time had arrived,
I was outside!
But who could I find?
My daddy arrived.

They put me in an incubator,
I shouldn't have been here
Till five weeks later.

So here I am, ten years on,
Full of life with wit and song,
Loving life,
Which makes me strong.

Abbie Hooper (10)
Oakfield Junior School, Fetcham

Music

Music is ever changing,
It comes in all different types.
Some is heavy, some is light,
Others waft through the night.
Classical music is sophisticated and quirky,
Opera is a test of human talent,
Jazz is to make people feel good,
Blues is to let them know how you feel,
Indie is to celebrate everyone's individuality,
And pop to change with the flow.

Katy Hart (11)
Oakfield Junior School, Fetcham

Seashore

The day starts,
A clear, crisp, sunny day.
Seaside town awakes.
One, then two, then three people,
Pitching their windbreaks.
Tourists dive in the sea
Like puffins on their only catch.
The beach now wearing
A spread of brightly coloured people.
Seagulls swooping high and low
Over the trash cans.
A number of boats speed
Up and down the stretch of water.
The sun, like a burning beach ball, gets hotter.
Fat men and super-skinny ladies lay
In the scorching heat, turning beetroot-red.
The lazy day comes to the end,
Crowds reduced to dots of people.
Dusk falls, the beach is left alone
And the sea sighs with relief.

Helen Hutchinson (11)
Oakfield Junior School, Fetcham

I Wish I Had A Pony

I wish I had a pony,
A brown, shire pony.
I would ride it every day.
I would call it Brown Beauty,
And groom it every day.
It would be a very well-trained horse,
My pony called Brown Beauty.

Anna Rose Wyeth (7)
Oakfield Junior School, Fetcham

Summer Day

Summer's started, the hills are glowing green,
The leaves are bright green.
I look outside, I see the sky,
I feel the shimmering breeze
With a few leaves flowing through the air.
On the hill are a few flowers
With petals of different colours,
Red, yellow, pink.
The sun is bright,
We have fun until it is night.
In the night the stars twinkle bright
Until the night has finished
And the morning has come.

Nicole Sergiwa (7)
Oakfield Junior School, Fetcham

Poppy!

Dogs are big and hairy,
They're sometimes very scary.
They need walks every day
And really like to play.

They're bouncy and lively
And always ready for fun.
They'll eat anything,
Even a bun!

My dog is called Poppy,
Her ears are so floppy.
I shouted with glee
When she came to see me.

Elizabeth Anne Cole (8)
Oakfield Junior School, Fetcham

The Alien That Came To Stay

There was an alien who came from Planet Nay,
Who just wanted to come and stay.

He knocked on my door when it was daylight,
I thought aliens only came out at night.

He had green beady eyes and yellow scaly skin,
Was as tall as me with a big wide grin.

I wasn't scared, he looked quite fun,
But then he started to eat my chocolate bun.

I saw he was hungry so I gave him some tea
And then we went on a big sight see.

He was amazed at the telly, scared of the loo
And he even saw himself on Dr Who!

I started to like him and called him Gnome,
But then he said he wanted to go home.

I wasn't sad when Gnome went away
Because he said one day that I could come to Nay.

James Eade (9)
Oakfield Junior School, Fetcham

Volcano

V ery hot at the top, the lava spits out
O ver the peaceful city below
L ow, the sky sinks
C overing the land, ash falls as it erupts
A aargh!
N o looking back, will we escape?
O range glow surrounds the houses.

Joe Blunt (10)
Oakfield Junior School, Fetcham

Summertime Is . . .

Summertime is really cool,
It's when we get to be off school.
I get to play footy with my dad,
I always score, which makes him sad!

Summertime is usually hot,
I get to ride my bike a lot.
We go to see grandma by the sea,
She loves to play crib with me!

Summertime is an ice cream treat,
Plenty of food for us to eat.
Holidays in a foreign land,
Warm blue seas and lots of sand.

Summertime is my favourite time!

James Cooper (9)
Oakfield Junior School, Fetcham

Banoffee Pie

Oh my, oh my, Banoffee Pie,
Oh how I like to ride so high.
Banoffee Pie is not for eating,
She is very good at competing.
On a good day she flies like the wind,
On a bad day she should be binned.
Walk, trot and canter is Banoffee Pie's thing.
Standing still would be good if only she could wear bling.
Banoffee Pie is my beautiful horse,
But you knew that, of course.

Lauren Morris (11)
Oakfield Junior School, Fetcham

Dragons

Dragons tall,
Dragons short,
Dragons fat,
Dragons slim,
Fire breathers,
Crystal eaters,
Jewel lovers,
Tall killers,
Short killers,
They kill men,
Women and children,
Man kills dragons,
Just the same,
Some are peaceful,
Some just like to kill,
Smoking, fuming,
Ready to rip man
Limb from limb,
Sitting waiting for battle,
To come to him to
Stomp them to death
For all who dare
Enter the dragon's den!

Matthew Wilkin (10)
Oakfield Junior School, Fetcham

Killer Whale

He swims in endless circles
In his concrete cell,
Anger fills his mind,
Misery as well.
He should be lurking in the ocean depths
Searching for a meal,
Gliding through the currents
Chasing after a seal.
He should be frolicking with his family,
Jumping in the waves,
His curiosity should have no limit
As he explores dark treasure caves.
He should be swimming on and on
Towards the open sea,
Jumping for joy at the very fact
That he's living wild and free.
But he's locked in a marine park prison,
Feeding on dead fish,
He performs tricks for money
For his owner's wish.
A social animal all alone
With only some tourist for a friend,
He stares at the wall and wonders once again,
When this life will end.

Megan Amis (10)
Oakfield Junior School, Fetcham

Space

Open air
Never stops,
Ties your stomach up in knots.

Giant fires
Light the sky,
Great big rocks pass you by.

Speed of light,
Seen by none,
Amazing sights for everyone.

Space is here,
Space is there,
Space is seen everywhere.

Megan O'Mahony (10)
Oakfield Junior School, Fetcham

Easter Means A Lot To Me

Easter means a lot to me,
The yellow chicks rise from their eggs.
Easter means a lot to me,
Eggs hiding and children hunting.
Easter means a lot to me,
Decorated eggs for all to share.
Easter means a lot to me,
Jesus dying on the cross.
Easter means a lot to me,
The Easter bunny hopping busily.
Easter means a lot to me,
With Easter bonnet parades.
Easter means a lot to me,
It is time to spend with your family.

Jacob Smith (10)
Oakfield Junior School, Fetcham

My Poem

I wrote this poem today, I wrote this poem myself,
I had this boring poem for homework,
I wanted to do something else.
I'm bored of using my brain,
Tomorrow I'm doing something,
So please don't rain!
The poem is rubbish, I'm sure of that,
My mum is watching football,
I wish I was doing what my brother is doing,
And he's catching a rat!
I wish that my brother had this homework
And I had maths,
I wish I was with my friend Cathy,
But we call her Cath.
So here I am at the end of my poem,
Finally I'm done,
So bye for now, that's so good to hear,
'Ride me, ride me,' my bike's screaming in my ear!

Sinead Robinson (9)
Oakfield Junior School, Fetcham

The Tiger

The tiger lays on the ground like a tree trunk
Waiting to catch his prey.
His coat as soft as a teddy bear,
His claws as sharp as knives,
His long tail like a snake.
His eyes as bright and as lively
As a playful kitten,
His nose as wet as water
And his teeth as sharp as
Razor blades cutting through things.
He camouflages himself
So no one can hunt him down
In the long, coloured grass.

Devon McDonald-Howe (9)
Oakfield Junior School, Fetcham

My Rabbit

I ran across the garden
As fast as I could.
I grabbed an apple in my hand,
My rabbit ran after me
As fast as it could
And bit my hand.
I was running away from my rabbit
As fast as I could.
My mummy came out and
Put a plaster on me
As fast as she could.
I picked up my rabbit and held it in my hand.
My rabbit ran after the apple
As fast as she could.

Katie Harrison (9)
Oakfield Junior School, Fetcham

Summer

Summer is a happy time
Where children dance all day.
You can get ice cream, yum!
But you have to pay!
Everyone can enjoy themselves
In the blazing sun,
Nobody will get angry,
There's always lots of fun
Seeing everyone
Playing on the beach!
Everyone enjoying themselves
In the summer heat!
I enjoy summer, I hope you do!

Sophie Way (9)
Oakfield Junior School, Fetcham

Mountain Peak

The mountain peak,
Trying to reach the skies.
Snow falling on the mountain's shoulders
Like icing on a cake.
And slowly eroding away
To the ground as a hill.

William Compton (10)
Oakfield Junior School, Fetcham

My Brother

My brother, Alex, is bigger than me,
He has ten legs but is frightened of me.
I can't lift him up, I've tried and tried,
I must look and see what's heavy inside.

Sam Chamberlain (10)
Oakfield Junior School, Fetcham

Dragon's Day

Fire dances in the smoke
While the smoke makes people choke.
His tail swishes in the air
While he knocks off people's hair.
He is the dragon from outer air,
Beware.

Sam Leyshon-Garner (10)
Oakfield Junior School, Fetcham

At The Mall

When I was two I went to the mall,
So much bigger than a market stall,
I saw them going to and fro,
A busy swing on the go,
But that was just an automatic door.
I thought I heard a lion roar,
Oh, that was just the man who announced
They were selling bananas by the ounce.
Then I heard a swarm of buzzing bees,
Actually it was people eating fish, chips and mushy peas.
All that time eyes had been looking down on me,
They were only the lights, you see.
It was getting late and I was tired,
But this mall had been
And adventure for a lifetime!

Kimberly Stiff (9)
Oakfield Junior School, Fetcham

On My Birthday

On my birthday I said,
'I want a telescopic bed.'

On my birthday I got a little robot.

On my next birthday I said,
'I want a telescopic bed.'

On my birthday I got chickenpox.

On my next birthday I said,
'I want a telescopic bed.'

On my birthday I got a puppy called Spot.

I'll have to manage without the bed!

Holly Seiver (10)
St Martin's Junior School, Epsom

Test Week

I detest the tests
That we have this week
It fiddles with my brain
I wish I could just run outside
And play in the pouring rain

I detest the tests
That we have this week
It mashes up my brain
I want to run away somewhere
Like Switzerland or Spain

I detest the tests
That we have this week
It tires out my brain
If I sit here any longer
I think I'll go insane!

Kyra Litten (10)
St Martin's Junior School, Epsom

Fireworks

Fireworks whizzing,
Fireworks fizzing,
Out in the night so bare,
Sparklers twinkling,
Sparklers sparkling,
Up in the cold night air.

Abi Cox (9)
St Martin's Junior School, Epsom

In The Summer

When the sun gazes down I know it is summertime again,
So I sprint outside, wrapped in my calf, mat, doves and stoat,
All snug as a bug in a mug.

I collect up all the sparkling purple snow in the garden
And start to make a snowman.

He gets bigger and bigger,
Soon he is so gigantic he is even smaller than me,
I stick two blue bananas for each arm,
A red pineapple for the nose,
Yellow ketchup for the mouth,
Then I put my mat on his head
And my red and green striped calf round his neck.

My two sisters and brother come running out
Ready for a boys versus girls snow pool fight,
At the start the boys are victorious
And the girls have lost.

Harry Symonds (11)
St Martin's Junior School, Epsom

Birthdays

I don't know why my birthdays
Never go according to plan.
It's always on my birthday
That everything goes wrong.

It may be the fact that my mum
Always forgets the candles
Or because my dad
Always wears his sandals.

Why, do you say that's the problem?
Because my birthday has been on
Wait for it . . . the . . .
28th of December for long!

Rosabelle Armstead (9)
St Martin's Junior School, Epsom

Glasses

My mum said I needed glasses
I'm not sure if I agree
Well who would want to see a man with a chart
And a first class degree.

The day came by,
Oh my, my, my.
It was my time to face the optician,
But why, why, why could it not possibly be a wonderful,
                                            tricky magician.

I sat in the chair
Full of despair
Wondering what I had done,
But believe me when I say this is not my idea of fun.

The minutes passed on
Until they were gone.
Then the man took a sip out of his cup,
Then said, 'As you knew there was nothing wrong for this was
                                            only a check up.'

Joshua Eastwell (11)
St Martin's Junior School, Epsom

School

Every day I'm always up,
But my mum tells me to wait,
I'm always ready before her
And that's probably why I'm late.

My teachers always get angry
Whenever I arrive after the bell,
They give me a good telling off,
No wonder it's called Hell.

Rhianna Miller (10)
St Martin's Junior School, Epsom

Moonlight

I saw her walking in the moonlight,
Her sad gloomy face made me feel sorry for her,
I could see the moon resting in her eyes.

As she turned to face a pool of midnight,
Hair swung down her back,
Her ebony-black cloak swirled around her feet,
Glistening with moon dust,
As she pulled back her hood revealing
A sparkling silver tiara settled on her head with
A symbol of the crescent moon on it.

I could see clearly that the icy wind
Was blowing on her pale face,
I thought I saw someone lumbering in the shadows,
It was spooky to hear the owls hooting
And the trees whispering secrets to each other,
In appreciation she sniffed the sweet smell of
The flowers and touched her silky petals.

An icy cold hand grabbed her shoulder,
She spun around and saw her long-lost sister Starlight,
I called to them but they ran off into the depths
Of the dark gloomy forest,
Starlight and Moonlight together.

Laura Sevenoaks (10)
St Martin's Junior School, Epsom

Starlight

I saw her walking in the night,
Her pale gentle face in the dark,
She looked at me out of coal-black eyes,
Yet they were shining like stars.

As she turned around her pool of midnight hair swung down
                                                                    her back,
She wandered around,
Her ebony-black cloak swished around her feet,
Glistening as I noticed the shimmering gold stars dotted everywhere,
I followed her keeping in sight the silk-grey dress woven with
                                                                     silver moons,
A tapping sound was made by her sleek, jet-black, knee-high,
                                                                     pointed boots.

It was clear that she felt the cold rush of the wind on her face
And saw dark shadows jumping about,
It was spooky to hear the owls hooting
And the whispering trees,
In appreciation she sniffed the sweet smell of flowers
And touched their silky petals.

An icy cold wind touched her shoulder,
She turned around and saw her long-lost sister Moonlight,
I called to them but they ran into the depths of the gloomy forest,
Starlight and Moonlight together!

Maryam Adil (11)
St Martin's Junior School, Epsom

Summer Holidays

Most years for our holiday
We travel far and wide.
Sometimes to new cities
Or places that we've tried.

But this year for our visit,
For all of us to see
Was outside of Europe
And off to Turkey.

The temperature was hot
For most of the day,
And what a relief
In the pool when we play.

The beaches were busy,
There were sports I could do
From windsurfing or jet ski
To banana boat too.

But best of all
Were the dolphins we rode.
I loved all the touching
And the tricks that they showed.

But two weeks were over
So quickly this year.
We returned back to England
To then shed a tear.

So it was back to school
For new things to learn
And maybe next year
To Turkey I will return.

Laura Foxley (11)
St Martin's Junior School, Epsom

I Love The Sky

I love the stars,
They shine so bright,
They're seen at dark,
But not in light.

I love the sun
And the warmth it gives,
It shines above
On all that lives.

I love the clouds,
They glide along,
They make me want
To sing a song.

I love the moon,
It glows with ease,
Even though
It's made of cheese.

Lydia Hallam (11)
St Martin's Junior School, Epsom

Gran

Fast knitter
Wet kisser
Good baker
Pill taker
Germ buster
House duster
Plate breaker
Leaf raker
Sherry lover
Wonderful grandmother!

Ruth Humphries (11)
St Martin's Junior School, Epsom

A Best Friend

Someone to rely on
Someone to care
Someone you know
Will always be there.

Someone to share secrets with
Someone to trust
Someone who knows
Why you don't eat your crusts.

Someone who knows how to have fun
Someone who is not mean
Someone to go to the movies with
Or to stuff your face with ice cream.

A best friend is precious
So don't let her go
You probably couldn't get on
Without her you know.

Scarlett Soodhoo (10)
St Martin's Junior School, Epsom

My Best Friends

Bryony's funny, Bryony's warm,
She cheers me up when I'm feeling torn.

Scarlett is bubbly, Scarlett is smart,
We're so close, you can't tear us apart.

Lizelle is crazy, someone you can trust,
Want to go shopping, the answer is a must!

Suzanne is sporty, I'm telling the truth,
She's so enthusiastic, she makes the best of our youth.

Our gang is solid, close as can be,
The key to our friendship, is locked within me.

Olivia O'Brien (11)
St Martin's Junior School, Epsom

Holidays

Holidays are fun,
Relaxing in the sun,
Splashing in the sea,
Dancing with glee.

Exploring summer resorts,
Prancing around in shorts.
Eating ice lollies
Under sun brollies.

Castles in the sand,
Listening to a band,
Making new friends,
Just before the holiday ends.

Holidays are *fun!*

Amy Ryckaert (10)
St Martin's Junior School, Epsom

Who Am I?

Cat eater
Bone chewer
Leg snuggler
Rabbit hunter
Sheep herder
Lamp post wetter
Fast runner
Kid lover
Burglar hater
Master protector
Fox menace
Postman chaser.

Sean Brown (10)
St Martin's Junior School, Epsom

Silent Night

Taking a walk,
Never guess who I saw!
The presence of night,
It left me in awe.

Her face I describe,
Drawn and pale.
Her teeth however,
Were yellow and stale.

Her hair past her shoulders,
All the way past her back,
Like an impressive curtain,
Straight and jet-black.

Her cloak wrapped her body,
It was ebony-black
And scattered with stars,
With a train at the back.

Evil and absent,
Her eyes were in slits,
Hypnotising and scary,
I nearly had fits!

Darkness behind
And daylight in front.
Making all children shiver,
Really is quite a stunt.

Chasing the sun
And its innocent glow.
Even sunlight can be put out,
By the terrors below.

Darcey North (10)
St Martin's Junior School, Epsom

The Wrong Way Right

The trouble is that left is right,
But right is never left,
And if you steal what is yours,
It's still considered theft.

If you circle round and round,
You never turn a bend,
But you're going straight forwards,
It tends to never end.

The sea is very dry today,
The desert very wet,
The ground is raining onto the sky,
The elephants forget.

Lauren James-Rikona (11)
St Martin's Junior School, Epsom

Chocolate

C runchy, crispy, chocolate sweetie
H ow I love it so
O h what a lifesaver my
C hunky chocolate dream
O range, mint and coffee flavour
L uscious, creamy flavour
A ddictive you just can't stop munching
T ongue tingling sensation
E nough is enough but you just can't stop!

Lauren MacKinnon (11)
St Martin's Junior School, Epsom

A Dog

Ball catcher
Flea scratcher

Bone gnawer
Loud snorer

Noisy barker
Cheeky parker

Selfish eater
Cat defeater.

Rachel O'Rourke (10)
St Martin's Junior School, Epsom

My Friends

My friends are wonderful,
My friends are cool,
They never say you're acting a fool,
They're always there for you,
They're always kind,
They always say what's on their mind,
They always help you when you're sad,
Or when you're about to go really mad,
My friends are funny, my friends are cool,
We always have a laugh at school.

Lizelle Johnson (10)
St Martin's Junior School, Epsom

The Playground

Greedy girls gobbling grub,
Sharing gruesome goodies,
Fabulous friends fussing around,
Choosing what game to play,
Terrible teachers terrifyingly
Ducking from flying footballs,
Boisterous boys bouncing about,
Being as silly as silly can be.

Danielle Owusu (11)
St Martin's Junior School, Epsom

Leaving School

Miss Sunflower's lot grew up,
Mr Musical's lot played away,
Mrs Car's lot boomed away,
Miss Dance's class danced out.

Mr Puff's lot puffed out,
Mrs Mouse's lot squeaked out,
Miss Dog's lot barked out,
Mr Cat's lot miaowed out.

Mrs Plane's lot flew away,
Miss Rain's lot ran off,
Mr Birthday's lot sang out,
Mrs Cow's lot mooed out.

Eleanor Charge (10)
Stepgates Community School, Chertsey

The Slaughterer

It slices strawberries,
Purees pears,
Bashes bananas
Without any cares.

No mercy!
Chop, chop, chop!
Gory glory!
It thinks the lot.

It is such a
Job to clean
The strawberry blood
From the machine.

It likes to see
The fruit scream out loud
Before it disappears
In front of the crowd.

Although it is the most
Savage creature
It has the most
Annoying feature:
An 'on' button!

Rudi Prentice (11)
Stepgates Community School, Chertsey

Sunflower

Slow grower
Water drinker
Light catcher
Sun watcher
Pollen keeper
Bee attracter
Energy keeper
Flower power!

Lewis Fry (8)
Stepgates Community School, Chertsey

The Athletic Pair Of Trainers

The pair of trainers lay
In a room surrounded by darkness,
Both athletes waited for their master,
As patiently as they could.

A blinding light shot into the room
And their master put a foot in each of them.
The two athletes walked to a field
That had other athletes in.

A crowd watched, cheering the heroes on
And got even louder
When the race began
And when our heroes ran.

Down on the floor
Our pair saw another pair,
This made tongues stick out,
Making our athletes zoom across the finish.

After this enjoyable race
Our winners climbed onto a podium
Along with the athletes from third and second place,
Our winner happily smiled at the sight of first place!

Peter Richard Robert Gerbert (10)
Stepgates Community School, Chertsey

Happy Or Sad?

Christmas makes me happy
Bullying makes me sad

Family and friends make me happy
But when I'm lonely that makes me sad

Baton twirling makes me happy
When I hurt myself that makes me sad

Seeing my nan makes me happy
Makes me happy when I'm sad.

Charlena Ward (10)
Stepgates Community School, Chertsey

The TV Set

I'm sitting in a cold room all alone but suddenly
There are children running round the room

They stop and turn me on
But suddenly there is a *boom*
I blow up cos I've been working overtime

I change my fuse
And give the kids a clue
About the mystery of the dew
They watch me long, they watch me far
I almost shout out to the house

We go and investigate the mystery of the dew
We find out that you can see them too
It happens at night in front of your eyes, the sky does agree
With us that we should know what's really going on in the world

The sun shines and shines sometimes
And Mum says go outside

If we were older we could stay up all night to see this happen
But we are only two
The telly says that it's time for us to rest our sleepyheads.

So goodnight!

Yasemin Carol Ann Kan (10)
Stepgates Community School, Chertsey

Fire, Fire, Bright So Bright

Fire flames are like sun's rays
But glittering in the night sky
Warming colours of red and orange
Sparkling through the haze.

Feel the warmth upon your skin
Making you sunny inside
Seeing the flames dance around
You feel the calm within.

Cheryl Jones (11)
Stepgates Community School, Chertsey

The Amazing Little Rugby Ball

At night,
It gets placed on a shelf,
By a human hand,
It's surrounded by lots of other equipment.

During the night,
It rolls like an excited child, opening his Christmas presents,
With this it tumbles down different levels like an elevator,
Finally it falls to the floor like a ton of bricks.

It meets another creature of its kind,
They both walk to see the sunset, like humans do in a romance.

They move back to the shelf, with no noise at all.
'Back to the shelf then for me,' says the ball.
And he is fast asleep before you can say Bob's your uncle.

Lewis Edward Hester (11)
Stepgates Community School, Chertsey

Pancake Day

Toss and turn
Fry the batter
Don't let it splatter.

Place the pancake on a platter
Sprinkle sugar, watch it scatter
Don't have too many you'll get fatter.

Yum-yum pancakes.

Bethany Neville (9)
Stepgates Community School, Chertsey

Seasons

Autumn
September, October and November:
Crunchy leaves underfoot.
Conkers falling from the trees.
Pumpkins and witches on Hallowe'en.
Guy Fawkes and fireworks on Bonfire Night.
These are the things that remind me of autumn.

Winter
December, January and February:
Short days and long dark nights.
Frosty breath and softly falling snow.
Brightly wrapped presents on Christmas Day.
The start of a brand new year.
These are the things that remind me of winter.

Spring
March, April and May:
Tulips and daffodils.
Hopping bunnies and skipping lambs.
New growth.
Hunting for chocolate-covered Easter eggs.
These are the things that remind me of spring.

Summer
June, July, August:
Long hot summer days.
Ice creams and barbecues.
Sandcastles and children splashing in the sea.
Happy holidays.
These are the things that remind me of summer -
My favourite season of the year!

Bethany Aira (8)
Stepgates Community School, Chertsey

Leaf

Tree liker,
Group sharer,
Nature finder,
Collage maker,
Share taker,
Tree finder,
Grass protector,
Green grouper,
Finder keeper,
Nature lover.

Asma Khan (7)
Stepgates Community School, Chertsey

Tree

Trunk bumper
Leaf faller
Wind blower
Branch cracker
Shadow catcher
Leaf blower
Long grower
Wind swayer
Types different
Rain catcher.

Lauren Melvin (8)
Stepgates Community School, Chertsey

Acorn

Leaf bumper
Dark jumper
Skin browner
Wind flower
Time slower
Water floater
Big thumper
Squirrel feeder.

Lillie Ella Derren (8)
Stepgates Community School, Chertsey

All About Me!

Face pinker
Baggy jean wearer
Chocolate eater
Duck, Duck, Goose player
Boy chaser
Party makeover
High School Musical lover
And that's up to
Me!

Ellie Evans (8)
Stepgates Community School, Chertsey

Flower

Sun trapper
Water catcher
Insect attractor
Pollen maker
Energy creator.

Charlie May Glue (7)
Stepgates Community School, Chertsey

Me

Big smiler
Red kicker
Furry coat wearer
Crispy fish eater
And that adds up to
Smiling, fish eating, football kicker, furry Mason!

Mason Page (7)
Stepgates Community School, Chertsey

Love Is Wonderful

Love is the colour red like Bolognese sauce.
Love tastes like sparkling chocolate.
Love smells like a cheeseburger.
Love looks like popcorn.
Love feels like hot steam on my head.
Love reminds me of food.

James Ellis (9)
Woodside Junior School, Croydon

A Happy Beginning

Happiness is a big red, bright ball rising in the sky.
Happiness sounds like a whistling through my head.
It tastes very warm like it has just been cooked in the oven.
It smells like freshly baked bread.
Happiness looks like people having fun in the park.
It feels like wind rushing through my fingers.
Happiness reminds me of trips.
Happiness is like mitts.
Happiness is cuddling up with my three dogs.
Happiness is like a heart pumping.

Martin Grady (9)
Woodside Junior School, Croydon

Darkness

Darkness is a pitch-black lonely crowd surrounding me screaming
and crying out my name.
Darkness tastes like liquorice melting in my mouth.
Darkness smells like a bright sparkling flame burning up
against my face.
Darkness feels like a damp shiver dripping down my body.
Darkness reminds me of a nightmare with a claw stretching down to
pull out my soul.

Georgia Doherty (10)
Woodside Junior School, Croydon

Happiness

Happiness is a rainbow lighting up the world like a diamond.
Happiness sounds like an angel singing a joyful song.
Happiness tastes like a bag of chocolates melting in your mouth.
Happiness is a ride on a helicopter on your first date.
Happiness reminds me of my first date.

Seyi Joseph (9)
Woodside Junior School, Croydon

Happiness

Happiness is like the sun shining bright.
It tastes sweet like chocolate.
It sounds like children laughing in the playground.
Happiness brightens up your day.
It is like a piece of chocolate melting in your mouth.
It reminds you of your happy time like when you first ride a bike
Or when your mum had a newborn baby.

Ryan Grace (9)
Woodside Junior School, Croydon

Love Poem

Love reminds me of my sweet family with a big red heart
that floats above your head.

Love tastes like a soothing and hot sausage roll
after a swim with my family.

Love looks like me and my family in the countryside
smelling roses and playing in the park.

At bedtime, love feels warm
and fuzzy with a hug.

Mason Ray Allen (9)
Woodside Junior School, Croydon

Love

Love is the colour of red strawberries being squeezed.
Love sounds like little robins singing in the air.
Love smells like golden fresh paint.
Love reminds me of the trips with my family.

Joe Burgess (9)
Woodside Junior School, Croydon

What Love Is

Love is a big red heart with me and my family floating around
 the Earth.
Love is my mummy singing like an angel from Heaven.
Love smells like Jean Paul on my mum's skin.
Love looks like me and my brother having a laugh.
Love tastes nothing better than my dad's spaghetti Bolognese.
Love feels cosy with my family.
Love is my sweet, sweet family.

Vanessa-Rae Harmony Williams (9)
Woodside Junior School, Croydon

Untitled

Darkness is like night following you everywhere.
Darkness is my heart, like the evil side of me.
Darkness is as black as space.
Darkness tastes like Brussels sprouts.
Darkness smells like a dirty bin that hasn't been emptied for years.
Darkness looks like a black graveyard and me.
Darkness feels like a black hole sucking you inside it.
Darkness reminds me of my dad giving me a good thrashing.

Mason Glading (9)
Woodside Junior School, Croydon

Darkness

Darkness is like a pitch-black night.
Darkness sounds like wolves howling.
Darkness tastes like banana flavoured medicine.
Darkness smells like smoke burning from a cigarette.
Darkness looks like blood spilling down your face.
Darkness feels like hatred pushing to the open.

Callum Harden (10)
Woodside Junior School, Croydon

Sadness

Sadness is the colour of blue like the sad sky.
It sounds like my mum crying for help.
Sadness tastes like horrible peppermints.
It smells of cold and hurtful feelings.
Sadness looks like a graveyard.
Sadness reminds me of sad things.

Chelsey Moran (10)
Woodside Junior School, Croydon

Hate

Hate is a stormy winter's day with no friends around.
Hate is a cold black shadow walking across my surprised face.
Hate tastes like Brussels sprouts at Christmas.
Hate sounds like screeching tyres on an icy road.
Hate looks like a shining skull in pitch-black darkness.
Hate is a feeling of icicles on my pumping heart.
Hate freezes my laughter and all of my hope.
Hate is a grey cloud raining sadness all over me.

Sophie Harrison (9)
Woodside Junior School, Croydon

Happiness

My happiness for football is when Arsenal win the Premier League.
My happiness is when I see my mum after school.
My happiness for my friends is having chocolate gateau.
My happiness for school is when I see my friends.
My happiness for going on holiday is when you jump in the
                                                  swimming pool.
My happiness for reading books is when I have fun.
My happiness for watching football is when Arsenal win!
My happiness for playing in a football team and winning!

Conor Wright (9)
Woodside Junior School, Croydon

Anger

Anger is a jet-black colour swerving around your head as if
                                    witches were flying about.
Anger sounds like adults screaming at children as loud as possible.
Anger smells like brown hearts rotting away.
Anger tastes like biting into a sour lemon.

Connor Moody (9)
Woodside Junior School, Croydon

Happiness

Happiness is a rainbow, lighting up even the darkness of places.
Happiness sounds like children running in the burning yellow sun.
Happiness tastes like a puddle of rich dark hot chocolate running
down my throat.
Happiness smells like an air freshener having sprayed around
the room.
Happiness looks like dark red roses growing in the middle of summer.
Happiness feels like the middle of summer with a light blue sky
and the yellow sun.
Happiness reminds me of a juicy bowl of fruit filled with apples,
oranges, pears and grapes.

Luke Majewski (10)
Woodside Junior School, Croydon

Love

Love is the colour red like your heart beating with joy.
Love sounds like a church choir singing a hymn.
Love tastes like hot chocolate on a floating cloud.
My love for my mum is the pink roses on a summer's day.
My love for my dad is a dream full of plays.
My love for my friends is like a Friday afternoon painting.
My love for my country is like nothing else.

Rejoice Mpokosa (10)
Woodside Junior School, Croydon

Happiness

Happiness is as cheerful as the bright sun on a crisp winter's morning.
Happiness smells like a Hawaiian pizza.
Happiness tastes like a ripe strawberry surrounded by my friends.
Happiness looks like a ginormous smile on their face.
Happiness feels like when you touch your pillow every night.

Aimeé Fowler (10)
Woodside Junior School, Croydon

Anger

Anger is as red as the Devil from the core of the Earth
Rising to your burning brain.
It sounds so evil you're tempted to attack,
It burns in your mouth,
It smells worse than burning wood,
It looks like death and a cloud of red smoke
Crawling around my frightened face,
It feels like coal,
It reminds me of my worst fear
Breaking into me like an eagle.
My anger was caused by a man taking my best friend.

Alfie Cooke (10)
Woodside Junior School, Croydon

Laughter

Laughter is a rainbow lighting up even the darkest place of life.
Laughter sounds like children playing in the happiest form.
Laughter tastes like the milkiest chocolate of the Earth.
Laughter smells like a crispy pizza cooking in an oven.
Laughter looks like hearts on a silvery plate.
Laughter reminds me of people telling the funniest jokes.
Laughter is spring and my brother, also somebody hugging you.

Scott Paul Wright (10)
Woodside Junior School, Croydon

Happiness

Happiness is bright and cheerful and is full of joy.
Happiness is as colourful as the rainbow.
Happiness is as bright as the colour yellow.
Happiness is as joyful as the birds.
Happiness is as joyful as the bright sun.

Renu James (10)
Woodside Junior School, Croydon

Darkness Of Death

Darkness is that tiny speckle of black hiding in every corner,
Every alley, in every dark night.
Darkness is the taste of sour bitter lemons squirting on your tongue.
Darkness is the sound of fear and sadness.
Darkness is black smoke covering your eyes filled with rage, hate
and anger.
Darkness is a smell of rotten eggs.
Darkness is your worst memory.
Darkness reminds you of death.

Luke Diboll (9)
Woodside Junior School, Croydon

Happiness

Happiness is as cheerful as the bright sun!
Happiness sounds like cheerful children!
Happiness tastes like a ripe strawberry surrounded by friends!
Happiness smells like a Hawaiian pizza in my kitchen at lunchtime!
Happiness looks like someone with a ginormous smile on their face!
Happiness feels like your pillow every night!

Isaac King (9)
Woodside Junior School, Croydon

Love

Love is all about families.
Love is the colour of glossy red sparkling in the sun.
Love is like the sound of angels singing from up above.
Love is the taste of chocolate melting in your mouth.
Love smells like a fresh touch of perfume.
Love feels like someone giving me a Valentine's card.
Love looks like a beautiful white dove.
Love reminds me of a family having a day out on the beach.

Simone Gordon (9)
Woodside Junior School, Croydon

Love

Love is like my friendship with my best friend.
Red like a rose from your true love.
Tastes like a thing you can't forget.
Feels like a hot cup of chocolate on a winter's night.
Looks like a heart running towards you.
Reminds me of love's first kiss.
Love is like a dream,
It's always with you.
I love the way it makes me feel.
My love and only my love.

Helen Alemseged (10)
Woodside Junior School, Croydon

Darkness

The darkness creeps on my back as I move swiftly.
The darkness is as creepy as the *Devil's* curse.
Darkness fills the room with silence except for the whispering in
　　　　　　　　　　　　　　　　　　　　　　　　　the distance,
A gentle gasp and I see a disfigured lady standing by me,
When I close my eyes and open them I see nothing but darkness,
As I turn around she whispers too, 'Farewell!'

Katie King (10) & Lauren Foster (9)
Woodside Junior

Love!

Love reminds me of the family that loves me.
It smells like a beautiful perfume on my mother's soft neck.
Love tastes like sherbet crackling in my moist mouth when my
　　　　　　　　　　　　　　　　　　　　　　sisters are there for me.
It sounds like happiness in the air when my dad is around.
Love is the colour of a heart lighting up your life when my brother
　　　　　　　　　　　　　　　　　　　　　　　　　looks after me.
Love feels like happiness everywhere I go.

Chelsea Couzens (9)
Woodside Junior School, Croydon

Who's Afraid Of The Dark?

Down a dark, dark city,
Down a gloomy road is,
Darkness.

Darkness sounds like
A wolf howling at the moon
And an owl hooting a tune.

Darkness looks like a haunted mansion
Deserted by its owners
And a hairy spider hanging from a cobweb.

Darkness smells like rotting corpses
Being gnawed at by hungry vultures,
Smoke rising from a burning fire.

Darkness feels like being alone
In a pitch-black cave.

Darkness tastes like a poisoned glass of wine
And a mouldy apple rotting at the dump.

Darkness is coloured black and grey
But when the sun rises it goes away.

Abby Furmston (10)
Woodside Junior School, Croydon

Darkness

Darkness is a pitch-black sky.
It tastes like slushy dark snow.
Darkness is a pitch-black sky.
It makes me feel cold and icy.
Darkness is a pitch-black sky.
It sends a shiver up my spine.
Darkness is a pitch-black sky.
When you're desperate and alone.
Darkness is a pitch-black sky.
And you know it's always there.

Telka Donyai (9)
Woodside Junior School, Croydon

Fear

As I stumbled through the wood at the dead of night,
The trees tried to grab me,
Snatch me,
As they slithered past my face.

Everything,
Silent,
Motionless,
Gloomy,
As the hours ticked by.

The wind howled and whispered in my ear,
Danger,
Danger,
As quiet as a mouse.

The moonlight was straining through the tree branches,
I ran faster,
Faster,
As the twigs snapped beneath my feet.

I was lost,
Frightened,
Lonely.

Luke Desmond James 10)
Woodside Junior School, Croydon

Happiness

Happiness is like a snowflake
Dancing to the ground on a winter's day.

Happiness is like presents
Arriving at your door.

Happiness sounds like a newborn baby
Crying when it is born.

Happiness is bright and fun
But happiness does not knock on the door for everyone.

Rebecca Hooper (10)
Woodside Junior School, Croydon

Who's Afraid Of The Dark?

In a dark, dark city,
down a gloomy street,
in darkness.

Darkness sounds like . . .
a wolf howling at the moon,
an owl hooting a tune.

Darkness smells like . . .
rotting corpses being gnarled at by witches,
smoke rising from a burning fire.

Darkness tastes like . . .
a poisoned glass of wine,
a mouldy apple rotting at the dump.

Darkness looks like . . .
a haunted mansion deserted by its owners,
a hairy spider hanging on a cobweb.

Darkness feels like . . .
being alone in a pitch-black cave,
having your last moment of life.

Darkness is coloured black and grey,
but when the sun comes it goes away.

Jamie Carr (9)
Woodside Junior School, Croydon

Be Afraid!

Afraid is a ghost
Swaying in the wind.
Afraid is like meat
Rotting in the bin
With rats gnawing at it.
It's a tarantula creeping
Up your back with its eight legs.
Afraid tastes like sour lime
With vinegar going down your throat.

Sanjay Ravindran (10) & Sammy Kiy (9)
Woodside Junior School, Croydon

I Can Never Stop!

I can never stop laughing
When my friend tells me a joke,
She often gives me a little poke.

A tear rolls down my cheek,
As it falls to the ground
I look up, it feels like I'm spinning around.

Laughter can hug you,
Such warmth, such happiness,
Your heart feels like it cannot stop.
That girl, Kayleigh, she cracks me up,
Until I go snap, crackle and pop.

Laughter is a cheerful sound,
It spreads joy all around.
We don't need any money,
Not even a pound,
We'll laugh forever with everyone together.

Daisy Boyle (10)
Woodside Junior School, Croydon

Silence

Silence is a whisper,
taken away by the wind.

Silence is peaceful,
as a feather drifting to the ground softly.

Silence is a pitch-black cave,
without a movement,
without a sound,
not a person in sight,
just me.

Ariana Andrade (10)
Woodside Junior School, Croydon

Silence

Silence is a holiday,
After a long term of work,
No people, just me.

Silence is as peaceful as a feather,
Drifting to the ground.

Silence is a black hole,
Leading to nothingness.

Silence doesn't speak,
It keeps its mouth closed,
For no one to hear.

Silence,
Silence is a different world to ours.

Bethany Jennifer Preece (10)
Woodside Junior School, Croydon

Terror

As the boy in his bed lay still he was silent,
Nearly everything was silent, the only movement was the rain
And the tree branches smashing against the windowpane,
The boy felt all alone,
Abandoned with the door locked like a bird in its cage.
As the hours ticked by,
At precisely 2am the moonlight rays beamed against his face.
Suddenly his window opened and whispered,
Danger!
Danger!
The boy instantly ran to the door, it was locked.
That's the end of that boy.

Ricky Parry (10)
Woodside Junior School, Croydon

Laughter

Everybody needs to laugh
Even if you're on the path.
The sun has to burst with laughter
And that's how it burns faster.
The moon jiggles and wiggles
As it giggles
When I see some holly
I get rather jolly.
Some people make me laugh
And make me cries tears of joy.
Laughter stretches around the world
And people fill with laughter.
As some people laugh
They stretch their necks like a giraffe.
Some people laugh and snort and laugh through their teeth
Just like the girl in Thornton Heath.
Some people laugh and everyone has to laugh
At something just like a hyena.

Elgiver Mame Pramei Acheampong (9)
Woodside Junior School, Croydon

Silence

Silence,
Is like a snowflake drifting to the ground.

Silence,
Is like a funeral march.

Silence,
Is motionless like a cloud floating in the sky.

Silence,
Says nothing she just stares at you.

James Clayton (10)
Woodside Junior School, Croydon

Happiness

Happiness is bright and cheerful, full of joy.
Happiness is wonderful, it's like a rainbow, colourful and bright.
Happiness is alive, free, free.
Happiness is like the birds dancing on a brisk summer's day.
Happiness is like Heaven.
Happiness is full of power.
Happiness doesn't come to everyone but to whom it does it will
last forever.

Alex Wade (10)
Woodside Junior School, Croydon

Happiness

Happiness is like a good thing in your life.
Happiness is like a present arriving at your door.
Happiness brings joy to the world and takes bad away.
Happiness is bright, joyful and fun.
Although happiness doesn't visit everybody
Some people are left out.

James Whiteman (10)
Woodside Junior School, Croydon

Silence

As silent as sitting on a beach in the middle of the night.
Silence is the moment you get your test results.
Silence isn't as loud as a feather falling on the ground.
Silence is as heavy as a gust of wind.
Silence is like floating in the middle of the night.

Ellis Brown (10)
Woodside Junior School, Croydon

Fear

I woke up, I was enclosed in a cold dark room,
Everything was silent except for the rustling of the leaves
On the crooked tree outside my window.
Immediately fear began to take advantage of me.
I reached out for my bedside lamp,
As I turned it on the light blinded me for it was as bright as the sun.
I got out of bed and as my foot reached the floor
The floorboard screeched like a macaw.
Then the light bulb shattered leaving me in pitch-black darkness,
Alone and afraid.

Joseph Bond (10)
Woodside Junior School, Croydon

Darkness

Darkness sounds like a fox screaming in the middle of the night.
Darkness smells like a bolt of smoke.
Darkness tastes like an extra hot chilli sauce.
Darkness looks like the deep, dark black hole.
To some people darkness is like walking in a graveyard.

Sheban Paramanathan (9)
Woodside Junior School, Croydon

Darkness

Darkness sounds like a screaming in the middle of the night.
Darkness smells like a bolt of roaring fire.
Darkness tastes like 100 million chillies.
Darkness looks like a deep, deep black hole in space.

Harry Jones (9)
Woodside Junior School, Croydon

My Anger

My anger is like a wind that crashes into
Every wall in my room.

I hate my friends, they get on my nerves,
They sometimes call me a nerd.

I feel angry because I can't get my own way.
It drives me up the wall every day.

Anger makes my sister cry and makes her fly,
Then say goodbye.

I don't like being angry, it makes me sad,
Then bad, then mad.

When I'm angry it spreads around the school
Which gets people into trouble.

Alex Isidoro (9)
Woodside Junior School, Croydon

Vicious Fears

The life drained out of me,
I knew I would soon die.
My heart sunk to the floor in pain
And eventually I would just lie.

As my eyelids began to duck,
My eyes erupted with tears.
The blood slowly ran down my arm,
I was full of vicious fears.

The night was as black as a raven,
There was a fierce breeze,
I collapsed to an expected death,
Falling to my knees.

Mia Brown & Bradley Sims (10)
Woodside Junior School, Croydon

Fear

As I sprint through the dark forest
the only thing that keeps me going is my own adrenaline,
fuelled by paranoia pumping through my entire body,
I feel petrified when the wind spits rotten leaves right in my face
and moonlight drips into the atmosphere.
I'm as scared as a baby without its dummy,
because I'm trapped in a world of phobia.

Jarrad Soundy (10) & Matthew Hacche (9)
Woodside Junior School, Croydon

Darkness

As I ran through the dismal woods,
The misty clouds darkened the sky
And the wind howled through the weak branches of the trees.
It was a nightmare!

The river was as murky as a swamp
And the grim voices in my head bellowed at me,
Telling me to run!
It deafened me as I was alone in the darkness!

Samir Barakeh (9)
Woodside Junior School, Croydon

Loneliness

I feel like the only person in the desert.
I can see only trees, branches, plants and mountains in the distance.
I feel like the only star in the sky.
I'm the only chair in the house.
I can hear the dust whistling in the wind.
The dust smells like mud.
I feel like the only person on Earth.
I feel soooo lonely.

Joseph Simon (9)
Woodside Junior School, Croydon

Dead Of Night

I trembled at the dead of night
When all monsters roam.
My heart turned to ice when
I realised I wasn't at home.

I dreaded going through a cemetery
Where all skeletons lie
Because it would have felt like going through a bat cave
At the dead of night.

Kobi Nanton (10)
Woodside Junior School, Croydon

Darkness

As I ran through the dismal woods
The misty clouds darkened the sky,
And the wind howled through the weak branches of the trees.
It was a nightmare!

The river as murky as a swamp
And the grim voices in my head, bellowed at me, telling me to *run!*
It deafened me, as I was in the darkness.

Millie Meilhammer (9)
Woodside Junior School, Croydon

Fear

I was walking in a park on my own at night,
With the rustling of the trees
And cracking of the leaves,
The howling of the midnight wind.

My heart is pounding like a big base drum,
Beads of sweat run down my face like a river,
I start to shiver as the wind brushes my hair like pointy fingers,
It was as scary as a horror movie!

Jack Kingsnorth (9)
Woodside Junior School, Croydon

Fear At Night

I was alarmed like a smoke alarm.
I was trembling with fear at the dead of night.
My heart was banging like a drum.
My hands were shivering like the wind whistling in the trees.

I heard a cry right round the side of Dead Man's Road.
My face was still, no movement came towards me.
As I ran and ran I feared I was not alone.
I felt like a wolf's prey.

Surraya Chowdhury Jhane (9)
Woodside Junior School, Croydon

Fear

I woke up, I was enclosed in a dark room,
Everything was silent except for the rustling of the leaves
On the crooked trees outside my window.
Immediately fear began to take advantage of me.
I reached out for my bedside lamp,
As I turned it on the light blinded me for it was as bright as the sun.
I got out of my bed and as I reached out of my bed the floorboards
Screeched like a macaw.
Then the light bulb shattered leaving me in pitch-black darkness,
Alone and afraid.

Dominic Richmond (10)
Woodside Junior School, Croydon

Loneliness

I heard the trees speak as I walked through the woods.
Then I knew that I was in the woods all alone.
The brown leaves cracked under my feet,
I felt as dead and as still as an ant.

Alexander Thomas Polydorou (9)
Woodside Junior School, Croydon

Laughter

Everybody needs to laugh,
Even when they're in the bath.
People sound like snorting pigs
Which make you do a little jig.
Laughter is as joyful as a new baby brother
And as lovely as I love my mother.

Hear the kids laugh and play,
It's funny in a silly way.
See the smiles run across their faces,
Hold their bellies and wriggle around the place.

The sun giggles when the moon jiggles.
The balloons burst with laughter
As the air is making a funny sound.

Laughter is so good for you,
It makes you happy when you're blue.

Kayleigh Hannah Long (10)
Woodside Junior School, Croydon

Happiness

You're a happy little bunny bouncing up and down.
You make me feel so glad with pride.
You're so high-spirited I get rosy cheeks like Rudolph's nose.
You're jolly, you're happy, you're like a cuddly bear.
When you were born you filled my eyes with tears.
You're as happy as a summer's day.
You're like a dancing tree.
You're as jolly as Santa Claus.
You fill my heart with love.
You're like a little roller coaster going round in my head.

Cheyeanne Nicholas (10) & Mollie Bailey
Woodside Junior School, Croydon

Anger

When my friend becomes angry
He just gives me the scares
I run away to the toilet
But he always beats me there.

When my friend becomes angry
I try to tell the teacher
But he always gets away
But some day I'm going to get him packing on his way.

When my friend becomes angry
He just plays badly so I don't deal with it and just stay away
He normally gets a few punches
But when the teacher comes he says he's not bad.

When my friend becomes angry
I get very frightened
So I keep away hoping he would
Be good another day.

Ben Lockett (9)
Woodside Junior School, Croydon

Fear

I sprinted past the motionless atmosphere as fast as my legs
could carry me.
Soon I tired to restrain myself from the monstrous thistles
So I could slip my feet out.
Later, I rapidly ran to another location.
Unusually, I found myself going over a waterfall.
I was so scared I thought it was a nightmare.
It led me into the water, looking at the waterfall with my eyes
barely open.
My head was at the bottom of the water near the currents.
I was terrified as something was taking the life out of me.

Shaquille Stephens (10)
Woodside Junior School, Croydon

Laughter

In the school playground the sound of laughter ringing through
                                              my ears,
Some people cackling like witches,
Others hissing like snakes,
A few children laughing and snorting like pigs.

In the school playground the sound of laughter ringing through
                                              my ears,
The trees giggling and shaking off their fragile leaves
When someone nearby tells a funny joke,
The sun laughing at the children being silly,
The football cackling when a team doesn't score.

In the school playground the sound of laughter ringing through
                                              my ears,
Children doing funny faces,
Friends telling each other silly jokes,
Others roaring with laughter for no reason.

The world would be dull and boring without laughter,
Everything would be gone, a few days after,
So have a bit of fun,
Otherwise the light will be gone.

Emma Dewsbury (9)
Woodside Junior School, Croydon

Happiness

Happiness is sitting around a warm cosy fire drinking hot chocolate
                                              on a dark, wet, icy evening.
Happiness is a family spending time together.
Happiness is a child playing in the sand at the beach.
Happiness is chocolate melting in your mouth,
It feels like it's oozing and dripping out your mouth.
Happiness is having enough food and water to eat and drink.
Happiness is having enough clothes to wear.

Lucy Day (9)
Woodside Junior School, Croydon

My Laughing Sister

Laughter can come from anywhere,
Especially if my sister's there.
She laughs and laughs and doesn't stop
And from her eyes roll teardrops.

My sister and I laugh together
And both will never stop.
She sounds like she's been hit with laughing gas
And it will never wear off.

Even when she's in her room
And I'm in mine
I can still hear her laughing
All the time.

Laughter will never stop
Even if my sister does.
My mum and I never get any work done,
She is a hyena that never stops laughing.

I love my sister very much
But sometimes she can over do it.
When she makes me laugh
I laugh, and I can never stop!

Brandon Basquine (9)
Woodside Junior School, Croydon

It's Taking Over

I'm in sadness all alone,
Closed up in this scary zone.
I know now what sadness is like,
It's like when you trip and break your new bike.
When it's dark and you're outside
And you just can't seem to find a tour guide.
When your friends and you break up,
Or when your mum shouts at you for breaking her teacup.

Jasmine Holder (9)
Woodside Junior School, Croydon

My Happy Feelings

Happiness is yellow,
It's yellow like my sister's clothes.
The sound of happiness is like children screaming at hometime,
Dashing left and right.
When I get happy I want to play, when I get too happy
I go hyper and mad.
Happiness is like having an extra person in my family.
Happiness is a friend trying to make me laugh when I won't laugh.
Happiness is when everybody laughs
And plays when everything is fair.
When I get happy I want to make other people happy
And want to play.
I feel delighted when I pass my spellings or get a new toy.

Dominic Summers (10)
Woodside Junior School, Croydon

My Mum

When I wake up and I see my mum,
My day fills up with so much fun.

My mum loves Christmas so much
She can't wait till the next one starts.

My mum and me go to the park,
To see the ducks till after dark.

My mum and me are just a friendship key
And it will never stop . . .
Well that's just me leaving my mum.

Georgie Jamés Newman (9)
Woodside Junior School, Croydon

Anger

What is anger?
Anger is when people clench their body
Like they are slowly letting air out of a helium balloon.
Anger is like a steam train inside your head,
Blowing steam out of my ears.
When your mother shouts at you constantly
And you can't take it no more.
Anger is like a bull screaming with anger,
When it is getting ready to charge before its attack.
Anger is when your friends wind you up
Like a wind up toy from the shop down the road.
Anger is when your face goes red,
Like you've just eaten a red hot chilli pepper.

Harvey Loundes (9)
Woodside Junior School, Croydon

Anger

Angriness is like getting out of control
Because it's very silly and dull.
Together we can change the world,
It would make me twist and twirl.
I see loads of people being narcissistic
But we all have different colours and faces.
                    I always see statues telling me,
                      'When I was younger I used to get bullied.'
                    I may not know who you are,
                      But deep down I know you are a star.

Daniel Boateng (10)
Woodside Junior School, Croydon

Me And My Sister

When my sister laughs,
I start laughing,
We laugh and laugh
And never stop.

We laugh for ages,
Just like hyenas,
When we stop laughing
The room is so quiet.

One of us breaks the silence
And the whole thing starts again,
We never stop laughing.

Veronica D'Souza (9)
Woodside Junior School, Croydon

What It Feels Like To Be Angry

Anger is like a screaming girl shouting in my ear,
Like when your mum and dad are angry you'll scream with fear.

Anger is a basketball bouncing in my brain,
If I carry on this way I'll go insane.

Anger is a crackling fire in my head,
Like when I hear fireworks as I go to bed.

I can hear my teeth grinding to and fro,
If I shake about my head will blow.

Anger is really nothing, you shouldn't need to worry,
Try laughing once in a while.

Sheneka Lindsay (9)
Woodside Junior School, Croydon

Fear In All Different Ways

Fear is at the end of every pathway,
It makes your head sway from side to side like a chameleon waiting
for its prey.
Fear is a contagious disease.
It sticks to you like bubblegum on your shoes.
You can't describe it.
You feel fear dancing around in your stomach like dancers
at Pineapple Studios.
It's like when a bully is trying to hurt you.
Watch out for fear once in a while.
Fear, fear in your ear,
Something that you don't want to hear.

Brianna Janel-Lindo (10)
Woodside Junior School, Croydon

Happiness

I am always happy,
I can feel it in my heart,
Even when I'm angry happiness is still there.
Happiness can destroy anger and darkness.
Happiness is what everyone is using most of the time.
I can smell happiness in the air.
Everyone loves happiness,
It's joyful and full of fun.
Happiness loves to be inside me.
Happiness is like you're on holiday for four months
With the boiling hot sun.

Kirk David Floyd Hutson (10)
Woodside Junior School, Croydon

Hunger

I am very hungry,
I haven't had anything to eat,
Nothing at all,
No fruit, no barley or wheat.

I am very hungry,
My belly's crying for help,
I don't have any energy to play
And I can't pay for food as I have no money.

I am very hungry,
My tummy feels like a black hole
Waiting to gobble up food,
I'm not being rude, but can I have something to eat?

I am very hungry,
I can hear my stomach rumbling like a lion roaring,
Waiting for his prey to come.

I am very hungry,
I feel sorry for myself,
But when I think, it could be worse,
With a tummy like a globe.

I am very hungry,
Maybe someone will come,
Give me some food,
Then I can be full again.

Robert Willard (10)
Woodside Junior School, Croydon

Me And My Mum

I love my mum
And she loves me.
We live together
As a family.

Sometimes we fight like two angry lions
But then it turns out alright.
We do everything together,
No matter what the weather.

We listen to the birds sing
And watch them flap their wings
Like beautiful rainbows in the sky.
We watch the sun say goodbye,
Then watch the moon say hello.

My mum is as caring as the Care Bears
And a love machine.

I love my mum and she loves me,
We'll be together for eternity.

Eleanor Clare Vincent (9)
Woodside Junior School, Croydon

My Hedgehog

My hedgehog goes out in the dark,
I am scared a ghost will play a prank on him.
I am scared he will bump into a panther
Because a panther is as dark as the night.
Some people think darkness is a pain
But other people think it is a gain.
I hope the moon looks down at my hedgehog
As he walks along the cobbled road
And then through the cat flap is my prickly little friend.

Ellen Lawrence (9)
Woodside Junior School, Croydon

My Bad Feelings

Anger is like a steam train in your head
And screams so loud when you're in bed.

Anger is like when you go to jail
And when you get out.

What is anger? I don't know,
It must have been a TV show.
Every day I have to moan,
I get no time to watch the show.

Ewald Hagan (10)
Woodside Junior School, Croydon

Love

Everyone has love for someone.
Love is like butterflies in my tummy,
As much as I love runny honey.
People love for different things like flowers
And chocolates more like my brother Billy,
He loves chilli.
When someone stops loving you it breaks your heart,
But love is always there for you even if you're not really smart.
Love is always around
And can always be found.

Henry Whiteman (10)
Woodside Junior School, Croydon

Laughing Sister

My sister is always laughing, she's driving me mad.
Then I feel very, very bad.

My sister always laughs through her teeth,
Like a snake hissing to say danger.

My laughing sister laughs in her sleep
Like a person snoring.

My sister hugs her teddy and gives a little squeak.
She jumps up and down and laughs right down to her little feet.

Dylan Offwood (10)
Woodside Junior School, Croydon

Darkness

It just struck dead of night
As I sprinted into the forest.
I couldn't see any light at all,
It was dark as my pupil.
As I looked around all I saw was darkness,
I didn't see the trees so I had to be careful.
It was like a pitch-black alleyway,
I couldn't see the end of the forest.
As I walked further, the arms of a tree swung
And hit me in the face.

Jake Michael Lawrence (9) & Nathan Hall (10)
Woodside Junior School, Croydon

Young Writers Information

We hope you have enjoyed reading this book - and that you will continue to enjoy it in the coming years.

If you like reading and writing poetry drop us a line, or give us a call, and we'll send you a free information pack.

Alternatively if you would like to order further copies of this book or any of our other titles, then please give us a call or log onto our website at
www.youngwriters.co.uk

Young Writers Information
Remus House
Coltsfoot Drive
Peterborough
PE2 9JX
(01733) 890066